TH

CELTIC
TAROT

INSTRUCTION BOOK

✠ ✠

THE
CELTIC
TAROT

INSTRUCTION BOOK

✛ ✛

JULIAN DE BURGH

ST. MARTIN'S PRESS
NEW YORK

Library of Congress Cataloging-in-Publication Data
available upon request.

ISBN 0-312-24181-X

First published in Great Britain by Rider Books/Random
House UK Ltd.

First U.S. Edition: April 2000

10 9 8 7 6 5 4 3 2 1

CONTENTS

THIS BOOK IS DEDICATED TO THE MEMORY OF
GEORGE ALPHONSUS MORRIS

ACKNOWLEDGEMENTS

The Celtic Tarot would not have been possible without the help of a number of people. I am for ever grateful to Catchie for her foresight, constant encouragement and patience in listening to my ceaseless chatter about the project. My mother Marie, who has always encouraged me to follow my dreams. My long-time friend Professor John Ryan, who never wavered when the going was tough. Reamonn O'Byrne for his wisdom and guidance. A special thanks to Una Morris who read and re-read my work and on many occasions put me back on the right track. My children Marc, Carl and Laura. Louise Brogan for being there when we needed her. Philip Morris, the man who inspired me to look beneath the surface, who is always in our memories. Last, but not least, Mary Guinan for the long hours she spent working on the wonderful illustrations.

INTRODUCTION

How to Use This Book

When I received the gift of my first Tarot deck, I was very excited and could not wait to get started – I planned to do readings for all and sundry. It was only when I sat down to start learning how to use the deck that I realized that it was not going to be as easy as I first thought. In desperation, I put the deck and instruction book away many times. A long time later, through trial and error, I finally grasped how to read the Tarot properly.

Having taught Tarot for a number of years, I realized something was missing from many of the instruction books available. When you either are given a deck or buy a deck, it is usually made up of two parts. These are the Tarot deck itself and an instruction book. This book usually gives you details of what the cards mean, and also includes a couple of layouts, but it does not include a step-by-step guide to putting it all together.

It is my intention in this book to take you through the steps of learning and understanding the Tarot. In the first section of the book, I deal with the process of learning the Tarot, and becoming familiar with the cards themselves. The second section deals with layouts and readings. Each stage is carefully structured to allow you to refer back and refresh yourself on any points you may have missed.

In the early stages of learning the Tarot, I recommend that you avoid trying to understand the deeper meanings. Get used to handling and giving basic interpretations of the cards first. As you become more proficient in and have more experience of reading the cards, you will begin to develop your intuitive and psychic side, enabling you to give more detailed readings. But all in good time.

Of course, it is only natural when you obtain your first Tarot deck that you will want to get straight into reading the cards, but be patient – take it step by step and it will pay off in the long run. Learning the Tarot can be an enjoyable journey of self-discovery.

CELTIC MYTHOLOGY

The fascinating ancient tales of Irish Celtic mythology are deeply embedded in the psyche of modern Irish society. Ireland's countryside is littered with thousands of monuments, all legacies of its ancient history. These monuments include dolmens – megalithic remains that are known in folklore as druids' altars. Then there are the *sidhe,* or fairy mounds, where the ancients were buried. It is believed that they are still inhabited by their souls, and also that the Tuatha Dé Danann (people of the goddess Danu) still live there today, thousands of years after they were driven underground by the invading Milesians.

One of the most famous of all historical sites in Ireland is Newgrange. Older than Stonehenge, this giant, megalithic tomb was probably erected around 3200 BC. It is one of a group of 40 passage- tombs that includes Knowth and Dowth in this area on three sides of the River Boyne. The mound was enclosed on the outside by a circle of standing stones of which 12 remain. This gives the impression that the monument was built and designed to stand out from the landscape – perhaps as a beacon for pagan worship. The present-day reconstruction, which is aimed at restoring the site to its prehistoric appearance, gives this theory further substance. The tomb is exactly positioned so that at dawn on the winter solstice a shaft of light penetrates the passageway and illuminates the inner chamber. The ceiling of this inner chamber is spiralled upward using huge stones that were stacked in a corbelled roof pattern. Inside are many etchings, the most significant of which is the one representing the sun. Nobody knows exactly what these designs meant to the original artists, why the tomb itself was constructed, and how it was so carefully aligned with the solstice.

Then there is the Hill of Tara – a magical place in Meath that was not only the seat of the kings, but also a centre of ritual significance. Apart from being a meeting place for kings and chiefs in time of war, tribal gatherings were also held there and ritual fires were probably lit there to celebrate Samain. Many of the tales of our past centre around this fabled spot. Golden torcs were found near the Tara churchyard in the early nineteenth century. The style of these torcs is consistent with ancient descriptions of dress at Tara. And, of course, Emain Macha (now called the Navan Fort) in Armagh, seat of the Ulster kings – and home to many of the feats and fables that centre around Cú Chulainn. Cú Chulainn, whose given name was Setanta, was the son of Sualdam mac Rioch, King of Cuailgne, County Louth and Dechtire, sister of Conchobar mac Nessa, High King of Ireland and Druidess daughter of the Druid Cathbad. As a youth Cú Chulainn went to Emain Macha to train with the Red Branch Knights and began the many adventures that have made him the best known and loved of all the heroes of Ireland's illustrious past.

The ancient sagas of Ireland are divided into four cycles of tales. The main source of knowledge of what has become known as pagan Ireland is the wealth of stories from the Mythological Cycle, which includes the great race of the Tuatha Dé Danann. The Ulster Cycle mainly revolves around Cú Chulainn and Emain Macha and is set in the first century of the Christian era in Ireland, around the time of the reign of Conchobar mac Nessa, King of Ulster, and Medb, Queen of Connacht. The Fenian Cycle centres on the reign of Cormac mac Airt, around the third century of the Christian era and many of these tales centre on Fionn mac Cumhaill and the Fianna. The Historical Cycle or Cycle of Kings is known as a mixture of 'genuine history with symbolic fact' and many of the myths are said to have their basis in historical fact. King Conáire Mór, a central character in the Cycle of Kings, appears on the lists of the Kings of Ireland.

However, it was not until the introduction of Christianity to Ireland that these fabulous myths and legends were recorded. Early Irish clerics – Christian but proud of their heritage – wrote down many traditional stories, epics and poems, including the Táin Bó Cuailgne (The Cattle Raid of Cooley). This is one of the most well-known tales of the Ulster Cycle,

involving Cú Chulainn and Queen Medb of Connacht. Because these stories had been passed on orally for hundreds of years, prior to their being
recorded by the monks of early Christian Ireland, there are as many ver-
sions of each tale as there are tales.

In the stories I have chosen to illustrate this Tarot deck, you will meet
heroes, heroines, gods, goddesses, human gods – men and women who it
is believed performed great and glorious feats. How many of them really
existed? We don't know. But they are part of our history and our psyche.
Even today in modern Ireland, many farmers will not tamper with or remove
an ancient fairy mound on their property.

Because of the nature and structure of the Tarot it is not possible to
place the tales in any particular order. However, these tales are not here to
give you a definitive history of Ireland and its people, but merely as a
descriptive tool to engage your imagination and perhaps inspire and guide
you in your understanding of the cards. Let your imagination take you away
to this mythical world of love and hate, lust and revenge. And hopefully,
as you get to know these fantastic figures of history and myth, they will, in
turn, help you understand the Tarot a little better.

WHAT IS THE TAROT?

The Tarot is a very old and sophisticated means of divination; its origin is
shrouded in mystery. Scholars generally accept that the earliest playing cards
originated in China and Korea many centuries ago. Unfortunately, there is
no evidence to reveal where or how the Tarot itself originally came into being.
We do know that the Tarot came into vogue in Europe as a card game in Italy
and France in the fourteenth century, and we also know it was used by the
Romany people as a means of divination. I believe we all have psychic abilities to derive meanings from particular layouts for a particular person or
question. It is important that you use the Tarot in a constructive and positive way, listen to and trust your intuition and you will never go far wrong.

At first glance the Tarot is very attractive and many are drawn to it.
They spend a lot of money buying decks and instruction books, only to

find a huge complexity of spiritual and psychological meanings. These interpretations are relevant but not at the early stages as they often put people off learning the Tarot. In this book, I have tried to keep the explanations as simple as possible.

Take plenty of time to familiarize yourself with the deck. By handling and using it again and again before even attempting to do a full reading, you will become more comfortable with your deck and the various meanings of each card. This will ensure that you will be more open to the intuitive guidance of the cards, and not just following the explanations given.

The Tarot Deck

The Tarot deck consists of 78 cards divided into two sections, the Major Arcana and the Minor Arcana.

The Major Arcana is made up of 22 cards, starting with the Fool and ending with the World. Their meanings are deep and refer to spiritual, psychological issues and more concrete changes unlike the Minor Arcana, which deals with everyday events.

The Minor Arcana is similar to the ordinary deck of cards, in that it is made up of four suits. However, each of the four suits has one extra card – the Princess.

The suits are:

Wands –   inspiration and creativity
Swords –   mental energy, strife and turmoil
Pentacles – material and financial issues
Cups –   emotions and affairs of the heart

It is also interesting to note that there is a correlation between the four suits and the four astrological elements, that is

Wands –   Fire
Swords –   Air
Pentacles – Earth
Cups –   Water

A Reading

While each card is interesting in its own right, on its own it is like a single piece of a jigsaw. It only gives you a part of the picture. It is only when you put an individual card into its position within a structured layout, and look not only at the card itself, but also at its position within the layout, and its relationship to the surrounding cards, that you see the complete picture.

There are two different approaches you can take to a Tarot reading. Firstly, you can do a reading related to a specific question. This is where a question is posed and you look at the issues directly related to and surrounding this question. Secondly, you can do an open reading, which is more common, where there is no question. This reading tends to highlight important influences and issues in the client's life at that particular time. The querent may or may not be aware of these issues.

THE CARDS

THE MAJOR ARCANA

Start by working only with the Major Arcana. Try to make this time of learning an enjoyable experience, look at it as a journey or an exploration of your inner self and your environment. Choose a time and a place that allows you to relax in peace and quiet.

PART 1

Study one card at a time. It is always useful to use a note pad to write down the points that stand out for you. Keep your notes as simple as possible. Sort the cards of the Major Arcana into the following order:

0. The Fool.
1. The Magician
2. The High Priestess
3. The Empress
4. The Emperor
5. The Hierophant
6. The Lovers
7. The Chariot
8. Strength
9. The Hermit
10. The Wheel of Fortune

11. Justice
12. The Hanged Man
13. Death
14. Temperance
15. The Devil
16. The Tower
17. The Star
18. The Moon
19. The Sun
20. Judgement
21. The World

Take one card at a time and, without referring to the instruction book, spend a little time studying the image on the card, keeping in mind the following questions:

How do you initially feel about the card?
What thoughts does this card bring to mind?

Try to identify with the positive parts of the imagery, that is the parts you feel attracted to, and then the negative parts of the imagery – the parts you do not like. It is important that you see both the positive and the negative sides of each card. Make some short notes on your initial impressions and then refer to the book and see how the Key Words relate to the images and to your notes. See if you can relate the card and Key Words with a particular issue or time in your life. Try to remember how you felt both physically and emotionally at that particular time. Take as much time as you need to become familiar with each card of the Major Arcana.

At this stage, you are only scratching the surface, as learning the Tarot is a continual process. As you practise and read the cards, the deeper meanings become clearer. I can honestly say that now, after more than 20 years of studying the Tarot, I still learn something new every day. Over the years, I have re-evaluated my feelings towards and interpretation of each card many times.

Part 2

You are now going to look at a simple three-card layout for the Past, Present, Future. This layout can be used for any question, but mainly focuses on general issues.

Shuffle the Major Arcana and draw three cards. Again, without using the book, study the cards in their positions. Taking your time, make notes on your thoughts on each card in its position and then refer to the book.

For this example, let's assume that you draw the following cards:

The Tower in the Past position
The Star in the Present position
The World in the Future position
The Tower (Key Words: Unexpected Change, Sudden Reversals)

In the Past position, the Tower indicates that unexpected changes have happened, and that these changes were outside your control. Plans that were built on a false sense of security come falling down. It can also indicate that change outside your control brings freedom from negative influences, people, places and environments.

The Star *(Key Words: Sense of Purpose, Inspiring Wishes, Dreams)*

In the Present position, the Star inspires you to reach for your highest potential. Even though negative changes may have happened as shown by the Tower, the Star of Hope inspires you to have faith in yourself. You can still reach your goals if you are prepared to redress and rebalance issues.

The World *(Key Words: Completion, Mastery over a Situation)*

In the Future position, the World indicates a very positive outcome, where you have brought together various aspects of your life. There is a sense of completion. The lessons of the Tower have been learned. Repeat this layout drawing different cards until you feel comfortable with it and are ready to move on to the next stage.

THE MINOR ARCANA

As we saw in the last chapter, the Major Arcana gives us important information, but using the Major Arcana on its own does not give us a complete picture. The Minor Arcana helps us complete the picture by supplying the missing detailed or everyday information. An easy way to learn the Minor Arcana is to understand the meanings of the suits and then blend them with the meanings of the numbers.

PART 1

We start this section by looking at the meanings of each of the four suits and then at the relevance of each of the numbers 1–10. We will look at the Court Cards separately in the next chapter. Taking this format, when you draw a Minor Arcana card you only have to think of the meaning of the suit and then the number, and then combining the two gives you a point to work from. This format certainly simplifies the meaning, but as I said earlier, as you become more proficient at understanding the basics, you will naturally develop a deeper understanding of the meanings.

The Minor Arcana is divided into four suits:
1. Wands
2. Swords
3. Pentacles
4. Cups

Each suit is divided into two sections:
1. The Numbered Cards, of which there are 10 in each suit
2. The Court Cards, of which there are four in each suit

Once again, I would like you to take time to familiarize yourself with all the cards of the Minor Arcana. As I mentioned earlier, the Major Arcana deals with major influences and the Minor Arcana deals with more mundane, everyday issues.

With the Minor Arcana, it is important to combine the influence of the nature of the suit with the number of the relevant card. You will see from the listing below that Wands represents Fire, Creativity etc., and an Ace represents new beginnings. Combining these two, we can then see that the Ace of Wands would represent the start of a new creative phase.

THE SUITS

Wands: The suit of Wands represents inspiration and creativity, an awakening, the vital life force. New ideas, a new outlook, a new creative attitude. Imagine there is a candle flickering away inside you, and suddenly it becomes fuelled with a new energy. There is a sense of physical energy and the motivation to achieve success.

Swords: Often seen as the most painful and sorrowful suit of the Tarot. Yes – it's true! Swords may indicate trouble, strife and turmoil, but they also indicate courage and mental energy, and the ability to instigate positive change.

Pentacles: Here we have the practical, material Pentacles, indicating finance and money matters. They represent physical and material goods and practical values; also physical possessions, and relationships.

Cups: Cups represent Water, the vital life fluid. Water in the Tarot represents emotions, and the importance of love in our daily lives. It is human nature to desire nurturing and caring. We hurt when we lose someone we love, either through the break-up of a relationship or through death.

THE NUMBERED CARDS

Aces: New beginnings

Twos: Partnerships, duality

Threes: Consolidation, the first stages of making new ideas work

Fours: Foundation, stability

Fives: Competition, instability

Sixes: Creative dreams at work, success

Sevens: Success against opposition, unexpected change

Eights: Positive or negative movement

Nines: Contentment, fulfilment, great loss or anxiety

Tens: Renewal, mastery

So, only using the Numbered Cards of one suit, and without referring to the instruction book, spend a little time studying the image on each card, keeping in mind the following questions:

How do you initially feel about the card?

What thoughts does this card bring to mind?

Try to identify with the positive parts of the imagery, that is the parts you feel attracted to, and then the negative parts of the imagery or the parts you do not like, keeping in mind both the value and the suit of the card. Make some short notes on your initial impressions and then refer to the book and see how the Key Words relate to the images and to your notes.

Then see if you can relate the card and Key Words to a particular issue or time in your life, trying to remember how you felt both physically and emotionally at that particular time. Repeat with each of the other suits of the Minor Arcana, and then you are ready to move on to the Court Cards.

THE COURT CARDS

Traditionally in the Tarot, the Court Cards represent people rather than situations or events. But this is not always true, so it is important that when reading Court Cards you look carefully at the surrounding cards, allowing them to guide you. If a Court Card is placed in one of the main positions, it can indicate the personality of the person. Or it can indicate that a particular person is going to play an important part in influencing the outcome of the question or situation. This may be positive or negative, depending on the card itself and the surrounding cards. One other attribute of the lower Court Cards, that is the Princess and Prince, is that they can also represent opportunities or news. Again this may be positive or negative.

Below I have shown some of the values placed on the Court Cards. Keep in mind, however, that a King does not necessarily mean a man or a Queen a woman. Nowadays, we see the cards in a more 'asexual' way. For example, we may see, in doing a reading for a man, that there are a number of very strong Queen cards. This can indicate that this person has strong traditionally feminine characteristics, e.g. a caring, nurturing temperament. Likewise for a woman, a very strong King influence suggests that this woman may have strong traditionally masculine characteristics. For the sake of simplicity, below I refer to the Court Cards as they are depicted, rather than the characteristics they represent, that is the Princesses and Queens are referred to as 'she' and the Princes and Kings as 'he'.

Again, take as much time as is necessary to become completely familiar with the Court Cards, as they are very important within a reading, particularly if they are in an influential position.

THE PRINCESSES
WANDS:

REPRESENTS An enthusiastic woman who is dynamic and creative. She enjoys living for the moment, loves challenge and is often the bearer of good news. MESSAGE It may be time to use your creativity and start in a new direction, no matter what your age. In a career reading it can indicate the offer of a job or a new opportunity to do with business.

CUPS:

REPRESENTS The opportunity to start a new relationship or partnership. It can also suggest the redevelopment of an old relationship or development of a present relationship to a deeper emotional level. MESSAGE The arrival of good news or news to do with the birth of a child.

SWORDS:

REPRESENTS A mentally active and highly skilled woman who stimulates new ideas and thoughts. Though not always grounded, the Princess can act as a catalyst and give inspiration to others who can take these ideas and develop them in a more practical way. In a relationship reading it suggests that you have a dreamy attitude to love and romance. MESSAGE News that indicates complete change for the better or worse.

PENTACLES:

REPRESENTS A reliable young woman who will not be easily distracted from her course of action. A good time to start a new job or change direction. The influence of someone who has good business sense or is financially sound. MESSAGE Good news about a new job, money or signing a contract. There is new a opportunity waiting for you, if you are prepared to look for it.

THE PRINCES
WANDS:

REPRESENTS An enthusiastic man who is dynamic and creative. He enjoys living for the moment, loves a challenge and is often the bearer of good news. In a career reading it can indicate the offer of a job or a new opportunity to do with business.

MESSAGE It's time to use your creativity and start in a new direction, no matter what your age.

CUPS:

REPRESENTS A man who is enthusiastic and open to new ideas. This man has a good understanding of his emotions and is probably offering the opportunity of a new relationship, or wants to develop a relationship to a deeper level.

MESSAGE Your present focus should be on creative, artistic abilities.

SWORDS:

REPRESENTS A man who is active and committed to developing his ideas to completion. It usually represents a young person with a quick mind, who has come or is coming into your life to offer you something. It may be love, an idea or an offer of some kind.

MESSAGE The arrival of someone who brings new ideas, one who would make a good friend, and equally a good enemy.

PENTACLES:

REPRESENTS A practical man who would be a good provider and family man. It can also indicate a man who brings practical advice to do with financial or property matters.

MESSAGE Good news coming to do with financial matters. You may need to seek advice from someone you trust on a financial matter.

THE QUEENS
WANDS:

REPRESENTS A woman with a dynamic, creative approach to life. She loves excitement and challenges in love, and can be spontaneous and passionate in romantic situations. The Queen of Wands describes a woman over 22 years of age, with a vibrant, outgoing nature. She acts on her feelings, is confident and enjoys action. She attracts many friends and her enthusiastic energy is a pleasure to experience.

CUPS:

REPRESENTS A woman with a loving and sensitive nature. She is gentle and kind and has a deep understanding of emotional issues. Guided by her feelings, she gives good, honest advice. However, you may not always like the advice she gives, perhaps because you know it to be the truth. Touch is an important part of her healing process and she loves to embrace. When in a crisis situation her healing energies are tangible, even at a distance.

SWORDS:

REPRESENTS A rational woman who is logical, with a well-functioning mind. She has definite ideas as to how things should be done, and is shrewd and mentally agile. She also has a careful approach to relationships and will be attracted by mental agility rather than looks or emotions. She tends to isolate herself due to emotional disappointments in her past.

PENTACLES:

REPRESENTS A woman who enjoys being a socialite and loves entertaining. She likes to spend her money carefully, is reliable and down to earth by nature. Her caring nature extends to all; she enjoys making others happy. Her advice is practical, and straight to the point. Because she is loyal and trusting, she will give you many opportunities to prove yourself, but if you do anything to lose that trust, you may never regain it.

The Kings
Wands:

REPRESENTS A man of strong principles who inspires confidence by his skill and his ability to get things done. He is a man with a dynamic, creative energy. His maturity and wisdom can be of great assistance to those under his care. He has a great dislike for routine, loves constant challenge and is a great starter of new ideas.

Cups:

REPRESENTS A wise and understanding man with a deep knowledge of the world. He is a caring, sincere individual who responds to the needs of others. Others turn to him for advice because they know his intuition is second to none. He is tolerant of views that are opposite to his own and will not be easily shocked.

Swords:

REPRESENTS A clear-thinking man who uses his mental abilities to pursue his goals. He is generally innovative in creating change, and is capable of pursuing many different goals at one time. He is an achiever who lays careful plans and makes sure they are followed exactly according to his system.

Pentacles:

REPRESENTS A man who combines knowledge and practicality to achieve his objectives. He is the builder and manager, a man who has achieved success through practical effort. He is intelligent and enjoys earning money. Material wealth is important, yet he is caring and a good friend. Sometimes seen as the banker.

THE FOOL

'Act now without concern for the risks '

KEY NUMBER: **0**

KEY WORDS

Adventure	*Excessive*
Freedom	*Insecurity*
Innocence	*Disregard*

UPRIGHT MEANING: The Fool represents spontaneous action, unlimited potential; you are now ready for change. Time to seize the day and enjoy it for what it is. The Fool can appear when you are about to take a risk, and the world around you warns caution. It indicates the enthusiasm that accompanies the onset of a new project or idea. Unaware of the pitfalls, you wish to embrace the future with great enthusiasm. It symbolizes the start of a new journey; you have to be prepared to take some risks to make big gains.

Reverse Meaning: In the reversed position the Fool indicates the desire to be free of responsibility. You are not prepared to take opportunities when they are there to be taken. The card suggests a foolishness in thoughts and actions, an unwillingness to take responsibility for the consequences of a particular action; an immature attitude to everything.

RELATIONSHIP MEANING: The card of the Fool represents a moment in your life when you meet someone new and something special happens. A spark ignites within and your very life force becomes alive, which can be so alluring that you are prepared go with it, despite the risks or consequences involved. In the reversed position, the Fool suggests that you are misreading your feelings or the intentions of another person. You may be looking at the other person through 'rose-tinted glasses' or fooling yourself about the other person's response in a particular situation or circumstance.

The Story of the Card: Setanta (Cú Chulainn) stands gazing at Emain Macha, the fortress of Conchobar (Conor) the High King of Ireland; he looks forward with a child-like, exuberant optimism.

Here we meet Cú Chulainn, one of the heroes of the Ulster Cycle of Celtic mythology. In his fifth year Cú Chulainn, or Setanta as he was known then, sets out alone to Emain Macha, to the place where boys and young men train as warriors in service to the High Kings. He gatecrashes one of the games where, surprised by his intrusion, the boys threaten him with death. He scatters and then defeats them with his amazing strength and skill. The five-year-old demands that the King put him under his protection and quite soon Cú Chulainn becomes the King's favourite. One day during the following year, Conchobar and his men go to a feast given by Culann the Smith, leaving Setanta to follow later. When the King and his entourage have arrived safely, their host lets loose the monstrous hound which guards his land, unaware that Setanta is still to come. Setanta arrives sometime later with his hurl and sliothar in hand, and is met by the hound charging towards him. Startled by the sudden attack, Setanta throws his ball with such force that it lodges in the throat of the hound, stopping him on the spot. Then, taking the creature by its hind legs, he flings it against a stone pillar, killing it instantly. Conchobar and his men rejoice at finding the boy alive, but the smith is saddened by the loss of his fearless watchdog. To amend the situation, Setanta assumes the dog's duty for five years, and from that day on he is named Cú Chulainn, 'The Hound of Culann'. His guardianship of the smith's domain symbolizes his future role as guardian of Ulster.

THE MAGICIAN

'I have the power to create'

FIRST CARD OF THE MAJOR ARCANA

KEY WORDS

Strong-willed	*Abuse of power*
Power to be original	*Hidden truths*
Ability to manifest your dreams	*Cunning ways*

UPRIGHT MEANING: The Magician has four tools available to manifest his will: the Sword of Intellect, the Wand of Inspiration, the Cup of Emotion and the Pentacle of Practicality. This card suggests that it is time to approach your whole life or a situation with a new creative and original attitude. The Magician tells you that you have the ability to act not react, you have the will-power to direct your energy in the direction you want it to go. With self-confidence you will gain the knowledge and the ability to tackle the important issues that need to be dealt with so that success can be achieved.

REVERSE MEANING: The Magician in the reversed position indicates a lack of confidence or loss of direction. In the reversed position it can also suggest that, up until now, you have not been prepared to use everything available to find a solution to a problem or issue. It can suggest that you are using deception, you are using your ability or situation to profit, or you are using others for the wrong reasons.

RELATIONSHIP MEANING: In a relationship reading, the Magician indicates that you have the courage and self-confidence to risk rejection and make yourself available and open to new relationship opportunities. You see the potential of a relationship and you understand what needs to be done to make it successful. In reverse the Magician suggests that your lack of self-confidence and sense of value is blocking your ability to open up to new relationship opportunities.

THE STORY OF THE CARD: The Magician, Mog Ruith of Munster, was said to be the most powerful Druid of Ireland.

This is the story of how Mog Ruith rescued the people of Munster from a terrible drought and famine, which the Druids of Ulster had sent in advance of an invasion by King Conor of Ulster. Mog Ruith ordered the men of Munster into the woods to gather rowan tree branches. When they returned, he told then to pile the timber into a huge heap and prepare to light a fire. When the timber was stacked and ready, Mog Ruith ordered each man to give him a shaving from the shaft of his battle spear. He mixed the shavings with magic oils and butter. He then lit the fire and, pronouncing an incantation, threw the mixture into the fire. Suddenly there was a huge explosion and a great ball of fire lifted into the air. Drawing the Druid's Breath of magical energy, a cloud blacker than black appeared in the air above the fire. Mog Ruith lifted his arms in the air, closed his eyes and began to chant a magic spell. Suddenly a ball of fire began to form in the flames and lifted into the air beside the dark cloud. As Mog Ruith continued to chant his magic words, the dark cloud and ball of fire merged into a single mass, causing a roar of thunder and flashes of lightning. It began to quiver and suddenly started to move at high speed towards the north. Conor and his men were making their last preparations when all became dark and heavy rain began to fall, thunder roared and lightning flashed until the forest around the camp burst into flames. Becoming frightened and confused, Conor asked his Druid for the meaning of the black clouds and the fire. The Druid replied that this could only be the work of the most powerful Druid in Eire, and that no army was strong enough to fight it. Overwhelmed by the great forces at work against him, Conor immediately called a retreat and his men moved quickly towards home.

THE HIGH PRIESTESS

'I trust my inner feelings'

KEY WORDS

Intuition	Shallowness
Hidden Knowledge	Superficiality
Depth and insight	Devious motives

UPRIGHT MEANING: The High Priestess suggests a heightening of the powers of intuition, and the ability to tap into psychic, intuitive levels, and to use this intuition as a means of guidance. You have a deeper understanding about a particular situation, without necessarily being able to justify where this sense or feeling comes from. You understand the importance of dreams, their interpretation and the messages they bring. The card also indicates the growth of a relationship on a spiritual level. It represents opposites: the opposites of reality where, perhaps, there is a strong physical attraction between two people and yet you know intuitively that this relationship will not work, without knowing how or why you know this.

REVERSE MEANING: The High Priestess reversed warns that you have not listened, or choose not to listen, to your inner voice for guidance. You are ignoring your intuitive guidance system, which could be telling you that unconscious factors are clouding or distorting the relationship. There is a sense of awareness, suggesting that you should consider seeking the help of a professional counsellor to help uncover issues hidden from your conscious mind.

RELATIONSHIP MEANING: Guidance and knowledge from a deeper spiritual level guide and inspire you in the development of your relationships. You have good judgement based on your psychic ability and you tend to trust your instinct, because it's usually right. You often understand, or are aware of, a psychic connection with another person, without necessarily having spent much time with them. In the reversed position, it suggests that some issues are hidden from your view, or that there is a feeling of deception – that someone is not telling you the whole truth.

THE STORY OF THE CARD: Ernmas had three daughters, Badb, Macha and Morrigu, together known as The Morrigan. The Morrigan was often identified with Anu 'the mother of the Irish gods' – a triad of Sorceress, War and Fertility.

The Dagda, the great god and magician of the Tuatha Dé Danann, was passing the River Unius in the county of Sligo to spy on his enemies, the Formorians, when he saw a woman washing herself in the river. He watched for a while before approaching her, and they talked before he waded into the river, where they made love between the rocks and flowing water. This woman was Morrigu, and after they had mated she forewarned the Dagda of an attack on the Tuatha Dé Danann by the Formorians. She advised him to summon all his warriors to the River Unius. By the time the warriors had arrived, she had captured and sacrificed Indech, a Formorian. She sprinkled his blood on the waiting warriors, as a symbol of the Formorian blood that would soon flow. As the warriors prepared to fight, she went with Badb and Macha to the Mound of the Hostages at Tara. Performing a ritual, they sent a rain of fire down upon the Formorians. During the battle she pursued and single-handedly killed all those who fled from the ferocity of the battlefield. She is also credited with forewarning Cú Chulainn of the Tain or the Cattle Raid of Cooley in which he would do combat with and kill his best friend Ferdiadh.

THE EMPRESS

'Nurturing and caring comes naturally'

THIRD CARD OF THE MAJOR ARCANA

KEY WORDS

Growth	*Despair*
Prosperity	*Failure*
Fertility	*Lack of productivity*

UPRIGHT MEANING: The Empress card suggests nurturing, caring, maternal feelings and fertility. There is a strong sense of being at home with your inner self, in touch with what is going on around you and at peace with the world. The Empress evokes peace, harmony – a woman who is not only in control of her femininity, but who is also wise and decisive. She is a person who is prepared to make sacrifices at her own cost for the benefit of others; one who inspires us to look at the greater good, and take all things into consideration when making decisions. When this card is drawn in a male reading, it indicates that this man is very much in touch with the feminine side of his nature.

REVERSE MEANING: The Empress reversed indicates difficulties in the home environment or difficulties within a relationship. It can suggest infertility or an unwanted pregnancy. There is a sense of domestic turmoil, or a lack of fulfilment. You can also be overtly protective of family and friends, and are sometimes accused of female dominance in a relationship.

RELATIONSHIP MEANING: You have very strong maternal feelings, with the desire to nurture and care for someone special, often with thoughts about pregnancy and children. It does not necessarily suggest that these feelings are being reciprocated, but the surrounding cards will give indications as to how the other person feels. In the reversed position it can indicate that you are not willing to give or capable of giving the support that a relationship requires; that you are lacking a level of self-sacrifice necessary to make this particular relationship work.

THE STORY OF THE CARD: Brigit: a goddess of fertility, a mother goddess. Her name comes from the old Irish meaning 'Fire' or 'Power'. Some records indicate that she was the daughter of the Dagda, a female sage, a woman of wisdom who married the Formorian King Bres. Other records suggest that she was Dana, the first great mother goddess of Ireland, who was later renamed Brigit and viewed as the sovereign, great mother who gave birth to all. She is associated with motherhood, fire, fertility and prosperity. The Celts had a very special bond with the earth, and treated it with great respect and devotion. They were also very conscious of earth magic, and understood that forests and rivers were to be held in great respect. Many shrines and places of worship were made in natural settings such as groves of trees, hilltops, wells and springs. Brigit kept a fire constantly burning at her place of worship in Kildare Town as a symbol of continuous life energy. The fire was looked after by vestal virgins. When Ireland was christianized, the pagan Brigit was adopted as a Christian saint. The fire was kept burning by the Christian Brigit's nuns until the twelfth century when it was extinguished by the Normans. Bealtaine was the celebration of the union of the earth goddess and her male consort, the balance between the male and the female and, in Ireland today, 1 February is still celebrated as her feast day. She is also credited with the St Brigit's Cross which is believed to be an ancient symbol for the sun and examples of which are still made today.

THE EMPEROR

'Do I need to control as I do?'

FOURTH CARD OF THE MAJOR ARCANA

KEY WORDS

Stabilty	Instabilty
Self-discipline	Lack of discipline
Authority	Heavy burden

UPRIGHT MEANING: The Emperor is a card of courage and ambition, established authority, and success through a self-disciplined and practical approach. A male/father figure, the Emperor has little time for emotions, but sees himself more as the provider of material things. This person enjoys working hard, and the rewards that hard work brings. When this card relates to an environment or situation, it indicates stability and a time of structure. This card suggests success in the material, male-dominated world.

REVERSE MEANING: Lack of self-discipline brings lack of success and too much control in a situation can stifle growth and limit movement and success. It can also indicate that he wants to ensure that things are done his way, whether it is the correct way or not and sometimes without regard for the fact that it is not the only way. He is sometimes accused of narrow-mindedness, or of being a 'macho' man.

RELATIONSHIP MEANING: There is a desire to take charge of a relationship, to establish rules and regulations within that relationship. The Emperor is not prepared to take no for an answer, and sometimes sees a relationship as a challenge in which winning is the only goal. In the reversed position, it suggests that you are not prepared to make any real effort to expand a relationship beyond its present boundaries.

THE STORY OF THE CARD: The Dagda: 'Good God' or 'all-Father' was one of the principal deities of the Tuatha Dé Danann – not always good in the moral sense, but good at everything. The Dagda's wife was called Boand. The River Boyne is named after her. The couple had several children, the most important of whom were Brigit, later known as Brigit the Earth Mother, Aengus, Aed and Cermad. The Dagda had magical powers and helped lead the Tuatha Dé Danann against the Formorians in the second battle of Mag Tuired. The Dagda carried a magic club so large that it would have needed many ordinary men to carry it. After a battle he would drag it along the ground, leaving an enormous furrow. Under the club, the bones of the Dagda's enemies were crushed. He also possessed the 'Cauldron of Abundance' – one the major treasures of the De Danann – which could never be emptied and from which no one ever went away unsatisfied. The Dagda also had a magical harp, which was stolen by the Formorians. With Ogma he set off in pursuit, and when they found it in the hall of the Formorian king, the harp was said to shriek with delight at the sound of the Dagda's voice and jump off the wall on which it hung. It then began to sing in praise of the Dagda. The Dagda became King of the Tuatha Dé Danann after Nuadu was slain by Balor of the Evil Eye at the battle of Mag Tuired. He ruled for 80 years. When the Tuatha Dé Danann were finally defeated, the Dagda led them underground to live in fairy mounds.

THE DRUID

'Guidance comes from above'

FIFTH CARD OF THE MAJOR ARCANA

KEY WORDS

Spiritual guidance   *Blind obedience*
Higher truth   *Bad advice*
Realization   *Error of judgement*

UPRIGHT MEANING: The Druid can be the symbol of the need to conform to rules or fixed situations. Guidance comes in a more spiritual way; there is nothing greater than the truth. There may be a need to seek spiritual guidance from one who is respected, or from a way of thinking that conforms to a specific framework. On another level, depending on the surrounding cards, it can indicate one is being guided by a spirit guide or higher guidance system, or conforming strongly to parental beliefs.

REVERSE MEANING: In reverse, the Druid can suggest an error of judgement. Rigid thinking leaves no room for growth. It can also represent the rejection of orthodox ideas and the formation of new beliefs. You may be following a particular path that others would not agree with and may even try and talk you out of.

RELATIONSHIP MEANING: The Druid shows a conservative and rigid approach to a relationship, or a relationship that must conform and be acceptable to a social or religious standard. It can be a union based more on stability than emotions. In the reversed position, it indicates the resistance to conform or commit to a conventional-style relationship, or the refusal to fall in with social or religious standards imposed on a relationship.

THE STORY OF THE CARD: The Druid seeks to find a connection between the higher spiritual level of the gods and that of men; he is in search of the truth. Druids or the priestly class were a race or sect independent from the other races embraced within Celtic mythology, yet they were very much interactive as advisers, magicians, seers, poets and civil judges. The Druids held a high office in the courts of kings as interpreters of the secret knowledge, and were always completely respected and believed. Druids put nothing down in writing, but spent most of their formative years learning everything in rhyme and committing the knowledge to memory. A trainee Druid would spend approximately seven years in training. He wore the robes of his office, and his rank and class were denoted by different bands of colours incorporated into his robe. The Druids were said to have used the entrails of sacrificial animals for divination. It is almost certain that the Celts used human sacrifice as part of their ceremonies and it is believed that some Druids would study the twitching, dying bodies as a means of divination. Other ceremonies involved human and animal victims being placed inside large, wickerwork figures and set on fire, and this practice was probably carried out in Ireland. Druids interpreted omens and were consulted by all to make decisions on timing and planning for all major issues and events, for example going into battle and marriage.

THE LOVERS

'The most attractive option is not always the right one'

SIXTH CARD OF THE MAJOR ARCANA

KEY WORDS

Decision	*Indecision*
Temptation	*Lust*
Moral choice	*Corruption*

UPRIGHT MEANING: The card of the Lovers urges caution: the most attractive option may not always be the best one to take. The Lovers shows a man torn between two women, a virgin and a temptress. It stands for tough choices, where moral values are questioned. To follow your own path you may have to go against those who are urging you otherwise; or go against conventional wisdom which suggests that your actions may be unexpected or unacceptable. It offers the option to develop a relationship beyond the relationship itself, with the possibility of higher goals and aspirations that two people can work towards together.

REVERSE MEANING: In reverse, the Lovers indicates the end of a partnership or friendship, or a situation that is destructive. You may be deluding yourself about your own motives, or the motives of others. You may be hampered by failing to see further than your own goals or desires, though this could be due to a fear of changing or going against the established order.

RELATIONSHIP MEANING: In a relationship question, this card can mean the process of having to decide between having to make a commitment to the relationship, or leaving it to follow a different direction. In the reversed position, it suggests taking advantage of someone for the wrong reasons, possibly for sexual fulfilment or self-gratification, perhaps due to a lack of self-esteem. It can also indicate that sexual issues are a dominant factor in your relationships.

THE STORY OF THE CARD: Cano was the son of a Scottish king who was forced to go into exile in Ireland. He spent his time there staying with an Ulster chieftain. Cano, the exiled warrior with a fearsome past, fascinated Cred, the Chieftain's beautiful daughter, and they spent a lot of time together. Slowly they fell in love. Cred wanted them to make love and tempted Cano many times. One night, she came to his bed and offered herself to the warrior who had won her heart. Though very much in love with Cred, Cano refused to make love with her as he was a warrior of honour, and an action like this would have violated the generous hospitality of the Chieftain's household. After a time, Cano was allowed to return to Scotland. Before he left Ireland, Cano and Cred pledged their love to each other and Cano promised to return as soon as he could to marry Cred. As a token of his love, he gave her his ring, whose stone held his very life force. He told her that she was now holding his life in her hands, and begged her to wait for him. For a very long time, Cred waited, but he never returned. One cold winter's morning, torn between despair and rage, Cred flung the ring to the ground, where it instantly shattered. As the pieces of stone fell apart, Cred realized what she had done – she had killed the man she loved – and her heart broke in as many pieces.

THE CHARIOT

'Take control and move forward with care'

KEY WORDS

Controlling a situation	*Loss of focus*
Strength of one's conviction	*Loss of confidence*
Dedicated to a cause	*Wrong use of energies*

UPRIGHT MEANING: The Chariot represents challenge. There is a need to remain focused and keep emotions in check. You may find yourself being pulled in two different directions when having to deal with a particular issue. You always try to overcome obstacles through perseverance and strength of will. You need to take control, harness your energy and apply it wisely. That combined with your usual search for excellence means that success can be achieved.

REVERSE MEANING: The loss of confidence or indecision in dealing with a situation can mean that you are stuck in a rut, or unable to move things forward. Remember that a lack of concern for others undermines leadership. You are sometimes guilty of allowing outside influences to dominate or control a situation, or failing to respond to the challenges that are being presented at the present time.

RELATIONSHIP MEANING: In a relationship reading, it suggests that there is some element of competition, or that competitive interaction plays a part in the relationship. Differences of opinion and attitude keep a relationship constantly stimulated. In the reversed position, this card indicates that one partner may be trying to control the relationship or one partner may fear being dominated by the other.

THE STORY OF THE CARD: The card shows Laeg mac Riamgabra at the front of Cú Chulainn's chariot; he drives the two stallions forward with precision and control. Each stallion, a powerful beast in its own right, instinctively wants to take its own route, yet in the hands of a master charioteer it submits to his control. To drive a chariot in battle, the charioteer must not only control his horses and his chariot, but more importantly, he must also control his emotions and trust his deeper knowledge. He may not clearly see which way he should next steer his horses, but he must stay in command, thereby ensuring that the horses stay under his control. Otherwise, these highly-strung creatures would panic and run wild, causing damage and even death.

Laeg was the child of a divine mother and a fairy father; he grew up in the Otherworld, the land of Tír-na-nÓg. As a grown man, he became Cú Chulainn's charioteer and also his devoted servant and friend, who proved his worth many times in battle. There were many omens to warn Cú Chulainn of his impending death, and one was clearly noticed by Laeg on the morning of Cú Chulainn's final battle. He saw the damage that had been done to the chariot by the Morrigan Goddess of War, who was trying to hinder his departure. As Laeg warned Cú Chulainn, his weapons fell from their rack. Cú Chulainn recognized this omen, and realized that he could not refuse to fight in the battle of Muirthemne. On his way to battle, he visited his foster mother to bid her farewell. After a long and bitter battle, Cú Chulainn, exhausted and dying, asked Laeg to lash him to a tree so that he could face death on his feet, and still fighting, braver than any other warrior. Laeg protested, instead wanting to help Cú Chulainn escape his fate. At Cú Chulainn's insistence, Laeg did as he asked, leaving Cú Chulainn to his fate and the Gods.

THE STRENGTH

'I must overcome my fears'

KEY WORDS

Courage	*Loss of courage*
Strength	*Intimidation*
Stamina	*Manipulation*

UPRIGHT MEANING: The card of Strength suggests that it is not brute strength that is now required. In fact, love and compassion are now required to bring about a solution to a situation. It does not mean that you do not have fears, it means that you are now ready to face up to them. It's time to tame the 'all-consuming lion' that lies within and is ready to consume you if you are prepared to let it.

REVERSE MEANING: At this level it represents an abuse of power, if in a position of power or control. It also indicates a loss of courage, or that you are giving in to your fears, which may be completely unfounded. You may be afraid to stand up for your rights or for what is rightfully yours. It can also indicate that you are giving in to your animal drives and are now becoming territorial. There is a suggestion of succumbing to lust, or sexual attraction, without thinking of the possible consequences.

RELATIONSHIP MEANING: In a relationship reading, it suggests that you now can overcome the fear of letting real love enter your life, and are at a stage where you can make a commitment. A current relationship seems to be based on understanding, with both partners being able to overlook the other's faults. In the reversed position, it suggests that one person is prepared to use the vulnerabilities of the other person for his or her own means. THE STORY OF THE CARD: Here we see the woman who has tamed the lion. Having found the courage to confront her fears, she is now able to bring them under control, and can at last find peace in the world. I like to call this lion the 'all-consuming lion' because it represents all our emotions and fears, or any combination of them. The lion is the royal beast and represents leadership, power and mastery. If we choose to let our fears or emotions completely consume us, they will take us over and we will always be at their mercy. But if we are prepared to tame them, through facing them honestly and courageously, we can overcome them and become inherently stronger. This card indicates that if you are ready to take the chance, you now have the strength, courage and ability to face your current circumstances, inner fears and desires. If you decide to use this courage to tackle your inner demons, not only will you be well rewarded, you may even find that these fears that have haunted you and prevented you from living a full life are completely unfounded.

THE HERMIT

'The answer is within'

NINTH CARD OF THE MAJOR ARCANA

KEY WORDS

Reflection	*Loneliness*
Truth	*Fear*
Guidance	*Sadness*

UPRIGHT MEANING: This card represents spiritual wisdom in the form of guidance from a higher plane. Some would describe the guidance as coming from a spirit guide or angel, depending on your point of view. This card indicates that it is now time for important reflection, when you need to step back and look for the answers or truths within yourself, and not keep trying to find them outside yourself. It can also indicate that it is time to seek the help of a counsellor to help unlock your hidden self.

REVERSE MEANING: The Hermit reversed foretells loneliness, sadness and delay. You may have a sense of being stuck in a rut, or perhaps you must face up to the fact that change needs to take place. You sometimes have a fear of looking within, and you can find yourself constantly seeking others who may have 'the answers' for you. On a physical level, you may be working in an environment where there is no social interaction, or where you somehow feel isolated or cut off from others.

RELATIONSHIP MEANING: In a relationship reading, the Hermit can signify that you need, even temporarily, to retreat from the relationship to see what you want and where you are going. You need to take time out to step back and examine your closest relationships with clarity and honesty. The Hermit in the reversed position can suggest that you may be misreading or choosing to misread the feelings and intentions of the other person in the relationship.

THE STORY OF THE CARD: The Hermit seeks solace, wandering among the stone idols on the lonely landscape of the Plain of Mag Slecht. In his hand, he holds his lamp in search of insight and understanding. The light from his lamp symbolizes the need to gain insight and understanding. The Hermit removes himself from everyday life so he can be alone in order to reflect. He understands that within every one of us, there is a need to withdraw from the main stream of life into a solitary time, seeking enlightenment. It is here he can be honest and true with himself, and tend to the needs of the mind and the soul. Clarity will come from within, that is if he is prepared to search.

Crom was a corn god whose stone idol could be seen on the Plain of Mag Slecht in County Cavan until 1900, when local folklore suggests that it was blown up by a local farmer. The Killycluggin Stone exhibited at the National Museum Dublin is believed to be Crom. It was said that there were 12 idols standing on the plain, all embossed in silver except for Crom who was embossed in gold. This was a special place for the Hermit to seek guidance because it was filled with spirituality and a sense of wonder. It was here that gatherings were held on the eve of Samain, when sacrifices of first-born animals were made. The gold-embossed idol Crom Cruach, one of the principal deities of early Celtic mythology, is also associated with the Mound of Crom Dubh. The Christian festival celebrating Crom's overthrow by Saint Patrick is celebrated on the last Sunday in July.

THE WHEEL OF FORTUNE

'Opportunities are now waiting'

KEY WORDS

Change	*Stagnation*
Good Fortune	*Misfortune*
Opportunities	*The unexpected*

UPRIGHT MEANING: You now have the ability to see the opportunities that are all around if you are prepared to stop for a moment to look for them. Life is in constant motion, and while you may or may not like where you are at present, you know that soon it will pass. This card indicates that your present circumstances do not have to be as they are. You have the potential to instigate changes now if you are prepared to do so. This card suggests the healing process.

REVERSE MEANING: The Wheel of Fortune in the reversed position indicates that some bad luck is about to come your way. If, however, positive cards surround it, you can rest assured that this will only be a temporary set back. In a business layout, the Wheel of Fortune warns of failure or loss of finances. You may need to cut your losses, and focus your energies in a new direction, where you will have a greater chance of success.

RELATIONSHIP MEANING: In a relationship reading, the Wheel suggests that your present emotional or relationship situation blends with your current needs or the needs of others. It also warns that you should not take for granted your present situation. If you are not in a relationship and desire to be in one, the opportunity can come at any moment. The same applies if you are in a relationship – you should not take it for granted. Things often change outside our control.

THE STORY OF THE CARD: The Wheel of Fortune is in constant motion. In this way it is just like life. Events can take a turn for the better or worse at a moment's notice and sometimes we have no say in what happens in our lives. No matter how well we plan ahead, the final decision is beyond our control. We may or may not like a particular situation that we find ourselves in, but one way or another it will pass and life will go on. The best we can do is to balance all of the elements at hand and make the most of what we have in any one moment. The only thing certain in life is that many opportunities will come our way every day. It is up to us to step back and take the time to recognize each opportunity for what it is and for what it offers. It is only then that we can choose to take or refuse it when offered.

JUSTICE

'I seek balance and harmony in all that I do'

ELEVENTH CARD OF THE MAJOR ARCANA

KEY WORDS

Mental clarity	*Dishonest dealings*
Balance	*Prejudice*
Peace of mind	*Complex legal issues*

UPRIGHT MEANING: The card of Justice indicates that you are reaching a state of balance. You are coming to a stage in your life or career where you can call on your ability to see both sides of a situation, and make decisions taking into consideration all the issues involved. Justice also suggests a legal decision in your favour. You realize that it's now time to be absolutely honest and take responsibility for your actions. In a partnership or business reading, it suggests a stable and calm environment in which both people understand each other and together make up a very efficient and balanced team.

REVERSE MEANING: You must now pay for your past actions. This could be in the form of a legal issue that drags on and will probably not give you the result you wish for. You are involved in an unbalanced situation, where there is a huge swing of either mood or attitude. There is deep conflict, disagreement or suspicion within a relationship.

RELATIONSHIP MEANING: The card of Justice suggests a calm and balanced relationship, which is generally free from conflict and disagreement. It also indicates that there is a level of understanding and acceptance of things as they are, rather than showing any desire to stimulate change. There is a sense of contentment. You may be moving on from a point where you went from one relationship to another just for the sake of change. Instead, you are comfortable and calm about your present state. In the reversed position, it suggests disagreements, quarrelling and a lack of communication. Justice in the reversed position also indicates that there could be legal action over possessions or property.

THE STORY OF THE CARD: The Midnight Court is the story of the poet Asling and his dream, in which he is brought before a court of angry fairy women, who live in a castle on a fairy mound. In his dream, he wanders through a beautiful countryside of rolling green hills, rivers and lakes, until he finds himself standing before the Midnight Court, representing the men of Ireland. The Court takes place in the main room of the castle. At the main table sits a row of large, round, buxom women who glare angrily down at him. One woman steps forward as prosecutor and accuses him and the men of Ireland of a reluctance to marry and make a commitment to the young, voluptuous Irish women. The only men who are willing to marry and procreate are the old, worn-out, sexually useless ones. As she makes this statement, a rousing cheer erupts from the crowds of angry women around him. One after the other, women from the crowd take the witness box and tell their stories of how the men of Ireland choose to ignore their needs, some sobbing, others angry that they never had the opportunity to have the children they desired. Suddenly the poet is seized by two women and dragged by the ear along the floor as the sentence is passed – he is to be flogged and made an example of. In a state of terror, however, he awakes from his dream.

THE ḤANGED MAN

'Rest now and let everything find its own balance'

TWELFTH CARD OF THE MAJOR ARCANA

KEY WORDS

Flexibilty	*Inner struggle*
Change	*Rigidity*
Meditation	*Disorder*

UPRIGHT MEANING: You know that to struggle now would serve no purpose. Be still, because now it's time to reflect on your past actions. The ability to adapt to changing circumstances can bring inner peace. It is time to focus on your needs rather than the needs of others. The secret of the meaning of your life lies within the self, and it is only through communication with the unconscious and feminine intuitive self, that you can find the answers to your questions and probably a lot more.

REVERSE MEANING: You find yourself submitting to the wishes of others, or being guided by what other people think rather than doing what is right for yourself. The Hanged Man can suggest a refusal to accept the reality of a situation, with a tendency to self-martyrdom on behalf of a lost cause. It can also suggest a desire to keep somebody in a partnership or situation for self-gain.

RELATIONSHIP MEANING: The Hanged Man in a relationship symbolizes the self-sacrifice that is sometimes required to make a relationship work, the ability to give and not always expect to receive. It implies the understanding that we sometimes need to put the greater good of the relationship before our own personal fulfilment or goals. In the reversed position, it suggests that one partner may be refusing to believe that a relationship is over, when the other partner has made quite clear that it is. Or perhaps situations are being created that force a relationship to continue, when it would be better to stand back and allow it to end naturally.

THE STORY OF THE CARD: The card of the Hanged Man is very symbolic. It appears that this man is to be sacrificed, yet in some way it also seems to be a voluntary sacrifice. His situation suggests a sense of suspended animation rather than martyrdom. In real terms, the Hanged Man represents suspension. He allows suspension of everyday life to get in touch with the spirit of his being, his pure unconsciousness. He abandons personal fulfilment and is prepared to sacrifice all he has accumulated up to now. By renouncing old values and material requirements, the Hanged Man is prepared to give up physical comfort in order to find a fresh purpose and a new meaning to life. Hanging upside down, he gets a totally different perspective.

DEATH

'It is time to let go of the old and look forward'

THIRTEENTH CARD OF THE MAJOR ARCANA

KEY WORDS

Change	*Loss of faith*
End of a cycle	*Lack of direction*
Fear of loss	*Inability to move*

UPRIGHT MEANING: The Death card represents the end of an era or phase in your life. It does not indicate physical death. The Death card tells you that the end of a cycle is now taking place. It may be a relationship, the end of a career position or an emotional cycle. It is time to mourn your losses, be happy with your memories, and allow yourself to move forward in peace. Change is often a blessing in disguise.

REVERSE MEANING: The Death card in reverse warns that to resist change will bring stagnation. You may be feeling stifled by guilt. This could relate to the death of someone close, the end of a relationship or a way of life. In some cases it can suggest the inability to let go and move on to develop a new relationship.

RELATIONSHIP MEANING: In a relationship reading the Death card indicates the end of an element of a relationship. If either the Tower or the Ten of Swords is in an influential position in the layout, the Death card can indicate the total end of a relationship. In the reversed position, the Death card suggests that a relationship has become stagnant or that one or both partners are resisting changes that may be necessary for the survival of the relationship.

THE STORY OF THE CARD: **Badb, the crone aspect of the triple goddess, is** associated with death or destruction. She is often linked with the Otherworld Banshee, as her wail warns of the death of someone close. She is also associated with battle and sometimes ran wild as a wolf among the fighting warriors. She is believed to preside over the boiling Otherworld cauldron of death and rebirth, where she decides the fate of those who live and those who die. It is also believed that Badb would cause the end of the world by letting the boiling cauldron overflow, flooding the earth and turning it into a wasteland. However, death brings rebirth and in the card we see four significant issues represented. The image of the person in the card represents you looking backwards, paying homage to the past, the good and bad times, which have to be mourned for but then left behind. The present environment is somewhat bleak and unproductive. We also see the river that must be crossed. On the other side of the river there are green pastures and a bright sun rising over the horizon, representing rebirth, the future, optimism, growth and development. It is time to deal with outstanding issues, emotions and baggage, you cannot move forward if you spend all your time standing still and looking back. The river represents the watershed – the letting go which will give you the freedom to move forward unburdened by the past, or by your pain, loss or hurt.

TEMPERANCE

'Open all doors of communication on a deeper level'

FOURTEENTH CARD OF THE MAJOR ARCANA

KEY WORDS

Interaction	*Unstable interaction*
Combination	*Conflict*
Flow of feelings	*Lack of communication*

UPRIGHT MEANING: This card suggests a spiritual relationship, a feeling of kinship with another, of being soul mates. Careful control will bring success. The card of Temperance indicates that there is a situation that requires deep communication to allow progress to continue. There is a need for communication on a deeper emotional level in a relationship. You must be prepared not only to talk but also to listen.

REVERSE MEANING: In the reversed position, Temperance suggests that you are not listening to what is being said. Not only are you ignoring what others are saying, but you are also ignoring the messages coming from your inner self. You have already decided on a particular path, or are in the middle of deciding something quite important, without reference to others involved or their opinion.

RELATIONSHIP MEANING: In a relationship reading, the card of Temperance symbolizes the mysterious chemistry between two people. It can often represent two people with very different personalities and perspectives coming together to create a unique, dynamic relationship. This connection blends the individual elements into a workable formula.

THE STORY OF THE CARD: In the Temperance card we see the goddess Bean Naomha. She is the goddess of wisdom, but the answers do not always come easily to her. She stands with one foot on a rock and the other in the water of the Well of the Sun, which lies in County Cork. She is content in all realms as she pours water from one cup to the other. She follows an ancient ritual of walking *deosil* or clockwise around the well three times, taking a drink each time she passes and each time laying a stone the size of a dove's eye on the rim of the well. Forming a question in her mind, she looks deep into the water for the answer. Her actions represent the need for the continual flow of emotions and feelings and the need for constant interaction in order to come to a final decision. In order to make a truly wise decision, it is necessary to look deep into ourselves and to take our time examining our emotions. Emotions are often changeable, even turbulent and violent, and not always gentle and happy. It is sometimes easier to disregard them altogether than to take an honest look at how we feel about a certain issue or decision. However, it is only by reflecting on all our feelings and emotions in relation to a matter, that we can truly find out how we feel about it and ensure that we make the correct decision in the end.

THE DEVIL

'I can untie the binds and set myself free'

FIFTEENTH CARD OF THE MAJOR ARCANA

KEY WORDS

Negative control	*Struggle for self-control*
Self-gratification	*Indecision*
Vulnerability	*Stagnation*

UPRIGHT MEANING: The Devil in this position suggests that you are being manipulated by negative, hidden influences. These influences may be in the form of a person who in some way controls your life. Or you may feel that, in some way, you are being controlled by your environment or even your own attitudes. You have a fear of taking your power back, and being responsible for yourself or your situation.

REVERSE MEANING: The Devil reversed indicates that you are not prepared to stay within a controlling situation. You are now seeking change both emotionally and physically. You are aware that you need to break free from the binds of the past and present, even though this may be difficult and painful to do. You are now strong enough to face the possible pain that this break will bring, and are willing to accept responsibility for your own life.

RELATIONSHIP MEANING: Within a relationship situation, the Devil can suggest jealousy or obsessive behaviour on the part of your partner. There may be an inner struggle or a sense of distortion that is controlling the relationship or situation. This card can also suggest that sexual attraction is the main factor in a relationship, and might in fact be the only factor binding the two people involved. In the reversed position, the Devil can suggest that you may be behaving obsessively towards another person in a sexual way; or that you are trying to control the other person's feelings and thoughts through your behaviour.

THE STORY OF THE CARD: Cernunnos (The Horned One) is the Greek name for the Pan-Celtic Great Horned God, the original Celtic name having been long since lost in history. Cernunnos was predominantly a stag god representing fertility and was a consort to the Great Mother. He was at his most powerful as the fertility god of the Bealtaine rites. As the Christian religion became more prominent, he was more often depicted as the anti-god Satan, an image developed in order to frighten people away from the old religion. Most graphic images of Cernunnos are consistent – he is nearly always portrayed with animals, in particular a stag or a serpent. He also wears a Torc denoting his noble rank in Celtic society. In mythology, the Serpent often represented pure knowledge. It may be because of his constant portrayal with a serpent that Christian monks associated Cernunnos with what they called the Devil or anti-Christ, since the serpent had been depicted in the Bible tempting Eve to eat the apple in the Garden of Eden. Because of his association with animals, Cernunnos is often referred to as The Horned God or Lord of the Hunt.

THE TOWER

'Change brings freedom'

KEY WORDS

Inevitable change	*Oppressive lifestyle*
Freedom	*Disappointment*
Enlightenment	*Obstructing beneficial change*

UPRIGHT MEANING: The Tower depicts inevitable change outside your control. Your present lifestyle, your attitudes or people in your environment are changing. Sometimes your subconscious creates change in order to free you from restrictions around you. In a health reading, it can indicate a sudden illness or shock that presents you with an opportunity to start a new way of life. Any major change can bring with it the possibility of freedom and liberation from negative influences, people, places and environments.

REVERSE MEANING: In the reversed position, the Tower augurs an incident which brings feelings of shame or scandal, or the sudden collapse of a relationship or business, or the loss of a job. It suggests unnecessary suffering or a disaster that could have been avoided. It can also indicate the reluctance to deal with or release yourself from negative influences or attitudes, or a restrictive or controlling relationship.

RELATIONSHIP MEANING: The Tower warns that even the most structured relationship must continue to grow and change. It cannot remain within rigid forms or boundaries. The Tower suggests a relationship that is under pressure and beginning to show strain as it is trying to accommodate the changing needs of one or other of the people involved. However, dealing with these changing needs will make the relationship stronger. In the reversed position, the Tower still indicates change, but this change is being resisted. Perhaps one of the partners is refusing to address the new requirements of the relationship, instead choosing to cling to the old ways.

THE STORY OF THE CARD: Balor of the Evil Eye was one of the most formidable kings of the Formorians, a race of people who invaded Eire. It was prophesied by one of his Druids that his daughter Eithliu would have a child and that child would kill him. To prevent this happening, he had Eithliu locked in the Crystal Tower on Tory Island, where she was to be attended on by only female servants and never allowed to set her sights on a man. Years later, Balor had his men steal a magic cow, which was owned by a Donegal chieftain called mac Kineely. The cow was brought to Tory Island so it would not be found. However, mac Kineely found out where the magic cow was and sent Cian, one of his bravest warriors, to Tory Island to retrieve it. Cian disguised himself as a woman and got to Tory Island, where he found the cow too well protected by Balor's warriors for him to reach it. However, he went to the Crystal Tower and, using a magic charm, was permitted to visit Eithliu. He left her pregnant and returned to the mainland. Eithliu had a son. When Balor found out, he was furious and took the child to the edge of the sea where he cast him out in a basket to drown. The child was rescued by a Druid and after many years of being fostered by Goibniu the Smith, he grew up to be Lugh, King of the Tuatha Dé Danann. In a later story, we will see that the Druid's prophecy came true and Lugh killed his grandfather.

THE STAR

'Inspiration is my guiding light'

KEY WORDS

Faith	*Rigid mind*
Renewed hope	*Self-doubt*
Quiet confidence	*Lack of confidence*

UPRIGHT MEANING: You have inner faith and the belief that you are following the right path. The Star represents the belief and hope that things will continue to improve. It shows that you are in a position where you are now able to give of yourself – 'letting the light out'– while being open to receive, allowing a flow of love and light to come to you as well as radiate from you.

REVERSE MEANING: In reverse, the Star suggests self-doubt and lack of faith in your abilities. There is a physical or psychological block that prevents you from moving forward. You are locked in by your inability to move beyond your present boundaries. You may be fearful of developing a relationship because of past disappointments or because of a lack of faith in people in general. Keep yourself well grounded and don't get carried away by fantasy.

RELATIONSHIP MEANING: The Star in a relationship reading can suggest that you may have over-optimistic expectations of the potential of a relationship. It may be that you are depending too much on your partner to fulfil all your expectations or wishes, instead of relying on your own powers and abilities. If you are not in a relationship, it can indicate that you have total belief that you will find a person with whom you can share your life and dreams. In the reversed position, it can suggest that you have doubts about the ability of a particular person or relationship to fulfil your expectations. It can also indicate a lack of belief in your own ability to develop and become a valid partner within a relationship, and this feeling is probably based on past experience.

THE STORY OF THE CARD: Caer Ibormeith was the Goddess of Sleep and Dreams. Like the card of the Star, she represents hope, dreams and inspiration. She was the daughter of Ethal Anubail, a fairy king from Connacht. Much poetry was written about her beauty and her powers of inspiration. Around her beautiful, white neck she wore a silver chain decorated with 130 golden balls. It is said that she lived close to a lake, and she and the rest of her clan often turned into swans and flew above the lake close to her home. Angus mac Óg fell in love with her in a dream, and he searched for many years before eventually finding her. When he did, he too turned into a swan. Together they flew away to Bruigh Na Boinne to make a new home and lived many happy, long years there.

THE MOON

'I can accept my deeper feelings'

KEY WORDS

Intuition	*Loss of nerve*
Powerful dreams	*Lack of confidence*
Subconscious messages	*Vulnerability*

UPRIGHT MEANING: The Moon is the card of nurturing. It represents strong dreams and powerful, intuitive messages reaching your conscious mind. Now is the right time to trust your intuition, even if it is in conflict with your common sense or with what those around you say. Some things are hidden from conscious view and it is often necessary to look well below the surface in order to find clarity and truth.

REVERSE MEANING: In the reversed position, the Moon indicates that everything may look all right on the surface, but there are many issues beneath the surface that need to be discussed and resolved. Uncertainty, fear and recurring feelings of negativity prevent you from dealing with issues that need to be faced now.

RELATIONSHIP MEANING: Strong dreams and fantasies are indicated when the Moon card appears in a relationship spread. Although you would like your current relationship to fulfil all your dreams and fantasies, there is no real indication that this particular partnership can do so. It could also suggest that even though you are in a relationship, you might be prone to dreaming or fantasizing about somebody else. In the reversed position, the

Moon suggests that you may be subject to very strong mood or emotional swings. This lack of control over your emotions can create unfounded fears and obstacles where there are none.

THE STORY OF THE CARD: The Moon symbolizes illuminating the hidden depths of the mind, the subconscious inspiration that stimulates the imagination. The Moon controls the waxing and waning of the emotions; it is in continuous motion and always reflecting a different light. Emotions, intuition and dreams bring to light issues of which we may previously have been only vaguely aware. The stone circle is real; it is there in stone, yet we fail to understand the depth of its true mystery and hidden knowledge. Light and dark alter the landscape. What is a comfortable landscape to journey in by day, at night becomes an intimidating place of changing shapes, frightening shadows and unfamiliar noises. The Moon illuminates this dark landscape, allowing us to see our way through the terror of the night. The Moon is constant and it is ever-present. Yet, every night it appears different, and allows us a new perspective.

THE SUN

'Optimism is a powerful energy'

NINETEENTH CARD OF THE MAJOR ARCANA

KEY WORDS

Optimism	*Proactive attitude*
Success	*Caution*
Triumph	*Stop daydreaming*

UPRIGHT MEANING: The card of the Sun represents energy, enthusiasm, taking care of the inner child and allowing spontaneity and openness to be an integral part of your life. The most optimistic card of the whole deck, the Sun offers happiness and inner peace.

REVERSE MEANING: In reverse, the Sun is still a positive card. Optimism is offered with this card, but there are doubts and a fear of being so optimistic, probably based on the experience of past failures. You may have a tendency not to take happiness at face value, and you don't always allow yourself to believe that circumstances are as good as they seem. You sometimes expect them to be mere illusions, and your contentment is sometimes overshadowed by the fear that the 'good times' can't last.

RELATIONSHIP MEANING: In a relationship layout, the Sun depicts a spontaneous, loving relationship that has balance, harmony and the potential for a successful future. There is a general feeling of trust and openness that is reciprocal. In the reversed position, it indicates that you are suffering from a lack of faith, either in your partner or the possible outcome of your relationship, when there is really no need for doubt.

THE STORY OF THE CARD: Lugh, the Sun God, was one of the main deities of the Tuatha Dé Danann and is honoured at the Sabbath Lughnasadh or Midsummer. Son of Cian and Ethine, Lugh was the grandson of the Formorian King Balor of the Evil Eye. After his birth, Balor had him cast out to sea, after it was foretold that Balor would die at the hands of his grandson. Lugh was rescued from the sea by a Druid and raised by Goibniu, the famous smith of the Tuatha Dé Danann, who with his two brothers was responsible for making the weapons for the warriors of the Tuatha Dé Danann. One story tells that Nuadu was holding a great feast at the royal seat of Tara. When Lugh arrived, he was refused admittance, and was told that only the most talented men of Eire were being permitted to enter. Eventually Lugh was able to prove to the gatekeeper that not only was he a man of one special talent, but had many skills. When he entered the great hall he was challenged by a harpist and asked to play. Of course, he met this challenge successfully and was given a seat at the King's table. Lugh later became leader of the Tuatha Dé Danann and led them into battle against his grandfather Balor at the second battle of Mag Tuired, or Moytura, County Sligo. When Lugh and Balor came face to face, Lugh hurled a powerful spear, made by his stepfather, through Balor's eye, pushing it out through the back of his head. This caused Balor's evil gaze to land on Balor's own men, killing all it shone on. Lugh was killed himself by the three sons of Cermait, seeking revenge for their father's death at Lugh's hands. Cermait's wife had fallen in love with Lugh and, in a fit of jealousy, Cermait challenged Lugh to combat. Because of a geis placed on him stating that if he refused a challenge of combat, he would be shamed as a coward, Lugh was unable to refuse, and killed Cermait.

JUDGEMENT

'Freedom from bondage awakens my soul'

KEY WORDS

Good judgement	*Loss*
Achievement	*Failure*
Accomplishment	*Recrimination*

UPRIGHT MEANING: You need to take an honest, unbiased look at where you are at present. Where you are now is a result of your past actions. It is time to realize that you are responsible for your own actions, though outside forces over which you have no control have impacted and will impact further on your life. A fair and honest appraisal will help you define clearly what it is you wish to achieve in the future, and the actions you must take if you are to have a chance of succeeding. By defining your goals and aspirations, you will be able to see the people, places and environments that will support you on your journey. It will then also help you to see the people, places and environments that will hold you back, or will be a negative influence on your journey.

REVERSE MEANING: There is a lack of clarity and a feeling of uncertainty about your goals. You sometimes have a tendency to waste opportunities, a sense of not being able to see the wood from the trees. You sometimes end up putting off making decisions or have a fear of making decisions, and this very indecision usually leads to loss and missed opportunities.

RELATIONSHIP MEANING: The Judgement card suggests that you have come to a point where you are prepared to take an honest look at your relationship for what it is, to a time of evaluation in which you confront issues that need to be honestly looked at. There is an opportunity to establish a relationship on a new footing. In the reversed position, it suggests that the partners in the relationship are refusing to accept responsibility for what the relationship has become; and there is a sense of denial or lack of commitment.

THE STORY OF THE CARD: Brehon laws take their name from the *breitheamh*, who were the lawgivers or judges of the Druid sect in Celtic mythology. The law was developed by the judges rather than by the rulers of the time. The Brehon judge interpreted the law and gave his judgement. He had to be careful when making a decision, because if he gave a ruling and it was appealed, he was liable for payment for his error, as well as having to forfeit his fee. Brehon law differed somewhat from modern law in that it was based on compensation rather than punishment. Capital punishment did exist but only in very rare cases. A 'blood payment' was the most common punishment imposed on someone who killed and could not prove that he or she had just cause to do so. The murderer had to pay a fine, or 'blood payment', usually of livestock, to the family of the murdered person. Another example of Brehon law was the trial marriage, which lasted for a year and a day, and after this time either party could decide to cancel the arrangement or make a permanent commitment. Under certain conditions, divorce was also possible and was widely used by both sexes.

THE WORLD

'I am co-creator of my world and all I wish for I can have'

TWENTY-FIRST CARD OF THE MAJOR ARCANA

KEY WORDS

Completion	*Unfinished*
Accomplishment	*Frustration*
Realization	*Struggle*

UPRIGHT MEANING: The World indicates the final and successful completion of any issue or issues in hand. It generally indicates that you have arrived at your destination; or have reached the culmination of a long series of events. It may also suggest travel in the physical sense, and always means great happiness and success. The World can also suggest that there is a dawning realization and understanding of where you are at, for the first time in a long time.

REVERSE MEANING: In the reversed position, the World suggests that the wonderful opportunities available are not being harnessed and are likely to be lost. You feel unable to complete a project or are struggling to find a purpose in a relationship. There may be a sense of denial – you refuse to accept that a relationship is already over.

RELATIONSHIP MEANING: In a relationship reading, it suggests that this relationship has now come to a point of completion and fulfilment. The relationship contains the potential and the dynamic energy that both people wish for. There is a positive end to a cycle.

THE STORY OF THE CARD: By comparing the journey of the Major Arcana with the Tree of Life, we see the structure of the Major Arcana. The card of the World is very symbolic in that it represents the completion of the journey that began with the Fool. This journey is one of discovery and learning, where we move through all the major events in the course of the Major Arcana. On our journey, we try to bring together the opposites of our being, the conscious and unconscious, the inner and outer world we live in, and our needs and the needs of others. This journey may not at times have been a pleasant one, and there are many lessons to be learned. The World is a very special card in that it suggests that these lessons have been learned and there is a sense of wholeness. However, the image of the hermaphrodite representing wholeness, as it is portrayed in the card of the World, is an ideal goal. It is not necessarily something that we can completely possess. We are human and therefore imperfect. However, when there is a sense of inner healing, and two disparate parts have been brought together, then you realize that a particular journey has reached its end. And so the next journey begins.

The Ace of Wands

Key words

New beginnings

Dynamic energy

Inspiration

Impotence

Blocked creativity

Over-confidence

UPRIGHT MEANING: The Ace of Wands suggests a new beginning, a creative, dynamic energy, and a spark of inspiration, which allows you to create a whole new plan for the future. The focus is on the potential of new ideas that are forming. You realize that you may have several options to consider, all of which look promising.

REVERSE MEANING: The Ace of Wands reversed suggests there is a block in developing a new idea or a new partnership. While you may want to move things on, you cannot find the inspiration or guidance to do so. You understand the need to harness and complete a project before moving it on to the next stage, but may be having a problem achieving this. There is a possibility that over-confidence may bring failure.

RELATIONSHIP MEANING: In a relationship reading, the Ace of Wands indicates the start of a new relationship, the development of communication between two people, or a strong psychical and sexual attraction which has the potential to develop. In the reversed position, the Ace suggests there is a lack of energy, passion or desire to develop a new relationship opportunity, caused by a lack of confidence.

THE STORY OF THE CARD: Bolga's Spear, or 'Gae Bolga', was named after the god Ailill Érann, who was also called Bolga. Also called the 'lightning weapon', it was made by the divine smith, a human god who made weapons for the Tuatha Dé Danann. It was recognized in mythology as probably the deadliest of all weapons used in Celtic Ireland. Cú Chulainn used the famous Gae Bolga when he fought for Ulster in the Tain, the famous Cattle

Raid of Cooley, and killed his blood brother Ferdiadh, who fought for Queen Medb of Munster. Medb, outraged at Cú Chulainn's refusal to become her lover, encouraged many young warriors to fight and kill him or die trying, offering bribes of land, bondswomen, and even her daughter Findabair in marriage. Finally, the desperate Queen realized that the only warrior likely to succeed was her champion warrior, Ferdiadh. Because of the bond between Cú Chulainn and Ferdiadh, both were unwilling participants in a combat in which one of them had to die. The combat lasted for three days, until a fatal strike from the Gae Bolga ended Ferdiadh's life.

THE TWO OF WANDS
KEY WORDS

Enterprise	*Avoidance of responsibilty*
Planning	*Procrastination*
The urge to move on	*Pessimism*

UPRIGHT MEANING: The Two of Wands indicates that you have come to a time of decision – you must decide whether you want to build on what you have or perhaps expand in a new direction. One part of you is content to stay in your present job or way of life and another part wants a change, a new direction and career challenges. It can also suggest that you may be in the planning stages of developing a new business. In an established business, the Two of Wands may suggest that you are looking at ways of expanding the current structure of your business or are in the process of developing a new direction.

REVERSE MEANING: Reversed, the Two of Wands suggests that you are afraid to move things on to the next stage. You would rather stay in a negative or unhappy situation or relationship, rather than force yourself to make decisions or changes. You should stop trying to justify why you should stay where you are, and put all your energy into taking on new challenges and opportunities, and seeing them through to their conclusion.

RELATIONSHIP MEANING: The Two of Wands suggests the development of a relationship that is based on physical attraction. This can often be a spontaneous interaction between two people, very much of the moment. It is often a relationship based purely on pleasure and passion. In the reversed position, it represents a relationship that is empty of love, where one partner has control over the other, or perhaps a relationship that is driven purely by sexual desire and pleasure, rather than by mutual respect.

THE STORY OF THE CARD: A Celtic farmer completes the building of his home, but there is still more to be done. This is only the first stage of a larger plan that will include pens and outbuildings for his animals. Unlike present-day farmers, the farmers of Celtic Ireland had no protection from raiders. A number of farming families would live together in small homesteads, groups of houses made of wattle and straw within a ring-fort. The walls of the fort were made of earth or stone and were up to six metres in diameter. Because livestock were a valuable commodity, Celtic mythology is littered with tales of raids. Some of these raids were highly organized, often involved armies made up of many hundreds of warriors and ended with huge loss of life, as in the Tain Bo Cuailgne or the Cattle Raid of Cooley. Another means of protection was homesteads built on natural or man-made islands called crannogs, surrounded by stone walls, some with one or two houses enclosed by a timber fence. In Lough Gara, County Sligo, during a drainage programme in the mid-twentieth century, over 200 crannogs were discovered. They are believed to have been inhabited until AD 1000. An unusual feature of some of the ring-forts was the 'souterrain', an underground passage that served as a hiding place.

THE THREE OF WANDS

KEY WORDS

Consolidation	*Wasting talents and skills*
Co-operation	*Delays*
The first stages of making new ideas work	*Set-backs*

UPRIGHT MEANING: This card shows a creative blending of energy. It represents the movement of ideas from the initial conception of the Ace and the planning stage of the Two to the point where action is now beginning to take place. It shows that there is co-operation from others, or that others are willing to help you make things happen.

REVERSE MEANING: The Three of Wands in reverse suggests that your efforts are being stifled. It is imperative that you pull back from your situation and review your plans objectively. You must obtain more information and not move things forward until you have established a more solid foundation.

RELATIONSHIP MEANING: The Three of Wands suggests excitement and passion between two people who are prepared to pursue actively similar goals in the development of a relationship. A relationship needs excitement and challenge to keep it stimulated. In the reversed position, the card suggests a relationship in which there is a conflict of interest, disagreements and probably a lack of direction. It can also suggest a partnership that is plagued with set-backs – perhaps a feeling that one of the partners is not being fulfilled by the relationship.

THE STORY OF THE CARD: Fionn mac Cumhaill stands guard on the ramparts of the tower on the Hill of Tara ready to fight the fiery Goblin whose magic music disarms his foes. Armed with a fairy spear, Fionn breaks the spell and slays the unsuspecting demon. The landscape in the card still looks the same today and shows the place where Fionn stood on that important day many centuries ago. Tara is regarded as having been the control centre of Celtic Ireland and it was the seat of the king from the earliest times. It was the most important centre of political and religious power in pre-Christian Ireland until the sixth century. *Lia Fail,* the Stone of Destiny, still stands on the Hill of Tara, though not in its original position. This small standing stone, only the height of a man, was the stone upon which the pagan kings stood at their inauguration. It was supposed to give a tremendous roar when a true king stood upon it. The tradition was that ritual fires be lit on hills and mountains all over Ireland on the eve of Samain (Halloween), the end of the Celtic year. It was prohibited for any other fire to be lit until the fire on the Hill of Tara had been lit and its light passed on to the surrounding hills and mountains. The light from these would be passed on in turn until all the ritual fires on every hill- and mountain-top were burning. Samain was a very special eve in the Celtic calendar, the night when the veil between the Otherworld and the world of the ordinary mortal was at its thinnest, and the souls of those who had passed over would come back to visit family and friends. It was, and still is, tradition that on this night food and drink should be left out for the visitors from the Otherworld.

THE FOUR OF WANDS
KEY WORDS

Recognizing a success
Milestone or special times
Accomplishment

Restriction
Lack of freedom
Oppressive situation

UPRIGHT MEANING: The Four of Wands often represents a stage where the first tangible successes are being achieved, and you are beginning to realize your ambitions. This is a time of negotiation, dealing with others and standing your ground. Your plans are beginning to come together. Numerous developments are occurring which will have a very good effect on your long-term plans. Now that the first stage has been achieved you can celebrate and move on to take up the next challenge.

REVERSE MEANING: In the reversed position, the Four of Wands suggests a sense of apathy – no matter how hard you strive for a particular goal you are unsure whether or not you are going to succeed, and sometimes find yourself unable to move forward. In a particular direction success seems to be delayed – as if there is a blockage preventing you from moving on to the next step. It is time to look at your overall attitude, or your attitude to a particular situation – a change of attitude may help things turn in your favour.

RELATIONSHIP MEANING: The Four of Wands suggests two people who are in a relaxed relationship, committed to each other and working towards the same goals. Positive interaction between these two people secures a solid foundation for the future. In the reversed position, it indicates a relationship based on low expectations and an acceptance of the limitations of the relationship. There is a sense of a lack of freedom or being in an oppressive situation.

THE STORY OF THE CARD: After the battle of Mag Tuired, the Tuatha Dé Danann for many years ruled a peaceful country. The fertile ground gave plenty of crops, so no one went hungry. In Spain, there lived another tribe of people called the Sons of Mil. On a clear day standing high in a tall tower on the coast of Spain, a magician called Ith thought he could see an island through a distant haze. Ith questioned his own vision, so each day for a week he climbed the tower and each day the vision became clearer until he could see beautiful mountains and forests on the island. He tried to convince his brothers of his visions and persuade them to go in search of the island, but they refused. However, fascinated by his father's vision, Ith's son joined his father and a few others and set sail for the island. It was a long and stormy journey until they finally came to one of the sheltered bays of the beautiful island. Ith and his men freely made their way to Aileach, the seat of the three brothers who shared the kingship of Eire. When he arrived at the royal court to offer friendship, he discovered the kings arguing over who had received the greatest segment of their dead father's land. Ith praised their beautiful country and told them they should not be arguing over small pieces of land when they shared such a bountiful and obviously prosperous country. He spoke at great length of the need for peace and harmony, especially among high-born men such as these brothers. Suspicious of Ith and his fanciful words, they planned an ambush and Ith and many of his men were killed. Ith's son managed to return to Spain with the few men who were left.

THE FIVE OF WANDS

KEY WORDS

Competition	Aggression
Irritations	Unnecessary arguments
Misunderstandings	Need for confrontation

UPRIGHT MEANING: This card represents competition, opposition, being against the odds. The competitiveness may be in a relationship where two people live separate lives and have limited time together. There is a need to gather your thoughts and have a look at your plans before proceeding again. You are struggling to succeed in a competitive environment. You must persist until you succeed.

REVERSE MEANING: In the reversed position, it suggests that you are more open to compromise and discussion. You have the ability to pull back from a disagreement and be more open to discussion rather than argue just for the sake of it. However, depending on the surrounding cards, it can indicate aggression. You may be focusing competitive energy in the wrong direction, wasting your valuable time and skills in unnecessary friction.

RELATIONSHIP MEANING: The Five of Wands indicates difficulties in a relationship because the people involved are pursuing different goals. These conflicts can often occur because one or both partners want to establish the relationship on their own rules and regulations without regard for the other person. In the reversed position, it suggests that you may be giving in to avoid confrontation and disagreement – and are unwilling to stand up for yourself or your beliefs.

THE STORY OF THE CARD: Lamenting Ith's death, the Sons of Mil returned to Spain and anger quickly spread throughout this country and the surrounding lands. Gathering many warriors, the Sons of Mil built up a huge fleet of 65 ships and sailed for the isle of Eire. When they arrived at the coast of Eire, the Tuatha Dé Danann were expecting them, but because there had been peace in Eire for so long, they had not prepared arms. In alarm the rulers turned to their Druids, seeking a solution. The Druids conferred and performed their secret rituals, and soon a fog began to descend over the entire coastline, and the land became shrouded in a soft, grey, blinding mist. The Sons of Mil became confused, and three times circled the island. Finally, however, a break came in the mist and allowed them access to the coast. Led by Amergin, the angry Spanish warriors made their way to Aileach where the kings were in council. Amergin informed the Tuatha that as a payment for taking Ith's life, they had to give over their land or fight to keep it. Allowing them time to decide, he said to them, 'We will go back to our boats and out over nine waves. We will come back over the nine waves, disembark and then take the island by force if necessary.' As soon as the Sons of Mil reached beyond the ninth wave, an immense storm seemed to swell from the very heart of the land. The waters turned to foaming monsters, the skies opened and the boats were thrown around in the water, many of them smashing on the rocks. Finally, Amergin made his way to the prow of the ship, where he invoked the spirit of the land of Eire. Instantly the seas calmed and the Sons of Mil made their way to the land. On the plains of Tailtinn, the dark foreigners met with the Tuatha Dé Danann in a fierce battle that raged for many days. Eventually the Sons of Mil overpowered the leaders of the Tuatha Dé Danann, and were named the new rulers of Eire. Led by the Dagda, the Tuatha Dé Danann went underground to inhabit the fairy mounds known as sidhes, and they have lived there to this very day.

THE SIX OF WANDS

KEY WORDS

Recognition	*False courage*
Achievement	*Short-term success*
Triumph	*Delay*

UPRIGHT MEANING: The Six of Wands indicates success, achievement. Problems are overcome. There may be recognition for this success from a greater spectrum of people than expected. This recognition may be in the public arena, and this level of recognition does not surprise you. However, a part of you may be wishing that this success was a little less superficial. It can also suggest that you are working in an area where public recognition is part of the job description, such as acting.

REVERSE MEANING: The Six of Wands reversed suggests that you may be giving up too soon. You feel overburdened and think that you have lost direction and focus. It can also indicate that you may be spending too much time focusing on your competitors' agenda and feeling threatened, rather than making your own more efficient.

RELATIONSHIP MEANING: The Six of Wands shows a well-structured relationship. There is further commitment to long-term plans, possibly a decision to marry or establish a home. This card suggests a relationship based on a mutual understanding of each other's needs. In the reversed position, the Six shows a lack of commitment. No matter what the potential of the relationship, there is a fear that the other person will not continue to work toward the common goals of the relationship.

THE STORY OF THE CARD: Nera's success in saving the court of Queen Medb and King Ailill is celebrated. It is the Eve of Samain, All Hallows Night, Halloween. And on this night the *sidhes*, or fairy mounds, open and the spirits of the dead come forth to move among the living. During the reign of King Ailill and Queen Medb on one such Samain eve, Nera, a servant to Queen Medb, is sent to Medb's torture house to tickle the feet of the prisoners hanging there. While he is there, one of the hanged men begs

Nera for a drink of water. Nera takes pity on the man and brings him to a nearby house where he drinks his fill. On their way back to the torture house, the man thanks Nera, and by way of thanks, tells him of a fairy mound, where Nera can find a magic woman who can free him from his servitude. Nera eventually arrives at the *sidhe* of Cruachain. After some time, Nera is offered a beautiful wife, and so decides to stay awhile at the *sidhe*. During his stay, he overhears plans to attack the court of Ailill and Medb the following Samain. Knowing he must return immediately to give word of this plan to Ailill, he asks his wife for proof of his stay in the *sidhe*, to ensure that he is believed. She gives him magic fruits that are found only in a *sidhe*. When he returns to his human wife and tells her the story of how he has been living in the *sidhe* of Cruachain and what is about to happen, she does not believe him. So he shows her the fruits. She persuades him to bring the proof to Ailill, which he does. Ailill is so enraged by the plan of the people of the *sidhe* to attack their court that he and Medb immediately send their men to the *sidhe* of Cruachain to destroy it.

THE SEVEN OF WANDS
KEY WORDS

Being aggressive	*Confusion*
Standing up for your rights	*Uncertainty*
Going after what you want	*Lack of commitment*

UPRIGHT MEANING: There are many issues to be dealt with at this time. You must have courage and not give up now as you have the ability to succeed if you are prepared to keep trying. Ensure that you consolidate your present position, so that you have both the courage and strength to succeed. From your perspective you sometimes see obstacles. However, in reality they are challenges that you are capable of taking on board.

REVERSE MEANING: The Seven of Wands reversed suggests that your energies are low and you cannot meet the challenges you now face. Be careful as you may be listening to the negative opinions of others and taking them as your own. You are letting them erode your confidence, instead of listening to your own instincts and finding your own way.

RELATIONSHIP MEANING: You are presently overcoming the difficulties that the Six of Wands presented. There is a sense of two people joining together to work out disagreements or differences of opinion. Both are committed to and prepared to work at making the relationship a success. In the reversed position, it suggests that one or both of the partners are letting the relationship slide: that there is a lack of commitment to overcoming the difficulties.

THE STORY OF THE CARD: Cattle raids were a regular occurrence in Celtic Ireland. A person's wealth was measured in part by the number of cattle he possessed. The infamous Queen Medb and her husband King Ailill, who had a passion for raiding the property of others, usually in order to steal an entire herd of cattle, instigated some of the most famous cattle raids. The story of the Tain Bo Cuailgne concerns a great war between Connacht and Ulster, centred around Medb's desire to possess the Black Bull of Cooley, owned by the house of Daire. This bull was attributed with great powers of fecundity. Medb and Ailill, in a contest to see who had the most wealth, found that they were completely equal, except for a bull possessed by Ailill, of which Medb had no equal. Medb sent mac Roth, her herald, and a group of nine to beg for a loan of this great brown bull, telling mac Roth to take it by force if necessary. However, when they were with Daire, they let slip while in their cups that Medb was willing to fight for possession of the bull. Daire was furious and sent mac Roth away empty-handed. When mac Roth returned to Medb and told her what had happened, she ordered an attack on Daire, saying, 'The bull, which is not to be got by fair means, must be got by foul; and by fair or foul, he shall be got by us.'

THE EIGHT OF WANDS

KEY WORDS

Progress	*Delays*
Movement	*Problems*
Satisfactory conclusion	*Insecurity*

UPRIGHT MEANING: The Eight of Wands indicates a feeling of positive, dynamic energy, which propels you forward. You may have sudden success or promotion to a new position that you desire in your career. It can suggest travel overseas. Goal-directed action will bring its own rewards.

REVERSE MEANING: The Eight in the reversed position suggests delays. You are not achieving the success you crave. It can also indicate that a relationship has not developed the way you would have wished. In a business reading, it indicates a partnership that lacks commitment from one or all parties involved.

RELATIONSHIP MEANING: In a relationship reading, the Eight of Wands describes passion and excitement in a happy relationship where you can enjoy life together without the need to struggle. It can also indicate you are planning an exciting holiday. This card may often indicate a change of direction and environment.

THE STORY OF THE CARD: Manannán mac Lir may be seen as the Irish Sea God, as his name means son of the sea (lir). Manannán appears in many of the old legends. He is a chameleon-like figure, who can change shape depending on circumstance. It is said that he travelled around Ireland in many different shapes and guises. He is often represented riding through the waves on his magic horse called Splendours Mane, and he is said to have lived on a number of islands including the Isle of Mann and the Isle of Arran. One image shows him as having three legs on which he rolled wheel-like along the ground, always surrounded by a magic mist. It is this three-legged image that is the origin of the Manx symbol, a three-legged wheel. Cú Chulainn fell in love with Manannán's wife Fand, living with her for a month while Manannán was away. Manannán appeared to Fand in a magic mist and shook a cloak between her and Cú Chulainn so that they would instantly forget each other and never meet again. One tale tells that it was Manannán who rescued Lugh as a baby when his grandfather Balor pushed him out to sea to drown. Manannán wrapped Lugh in his vast cloak and brought him to his Otherworld home beyond the sea. He was also seen as the Ferryman, who transported the souls of dead warriors through the magic mists to the lands that lay beyond death. A few brave warriors had the power to go to these lands and return to the living world to tell the tale. While out walking one day, King Cormac saw a boy holding a silver branch with three golden apples on it; this branch, when shaken, would play magical lullabies that lulled mortals asleep. The boy revealed himself to be Manannán. Cormac went with the boy to the Land of Promise where he was shown the Well of Knowledge from which five streams were flowing. Hanging over the Well of Knowledge were nine purple hazel trees. Five salmon in the streams were eating the hazelnuts. Manannán revealed to Cormac the meaning of all these wonders. Cormac was allowed to return to the land of mortal men with this wonderful knowledge.

THE NINE OF WANDS
KEY WORDS

Preparation	*Opposition*
Foresight	*Confusion*
Cautious attitude	*Avoidable loss*

UPRIGHT MEANING: The Nine of Wands suggests that now is a time to hold back or wait to consider and weigh up the odds. You need to be careful as you proceed, it is time to think carefully before making your next move. Lessons from the past will give you insight into dealing with an upcoming situation or conflict. In a relationship reading, it suggests that you need to examine your commitment, based on issues that have recently come to light. You must learn from your past mistakes.

REVERSE MEANING: The Nine of Wands in the reversed position indicates an inability to deal with issues that need to be confronted. There is a possibility, or you feel that there is a possibility, that you will lose your job or find yourself caught up in a situation you cannot find your way out of. You are very frightened of things happening beyond your control, or that you will not adapt to changing circumstances.

RELATIONSHIP MEANING: The Nine of Wands in a relationship spread suggests that this relationship has come up against some difficulties. However, these difficulties can be overcome if both partners are prepared to make a joint effort. In the reversed position, the partners in the relationship are unable to deal with their present difficulties and it seems that there is no clear solution. In this position, the Nine can suggest that the people in the relationship are no longer as compatible as they were, that one or both of them have changed or grown out of the relationship.

THE STORY OF THE CARD: The Tuatha Dé Danann came from the Northern Isles of the world, and when they arrived at Sligo on the west coast of Eire, they brought with them knowledge, warrior skills and wizardry far beyond those ever seen in Eire before. Mag Tuired was the scene of the two most important battles of Tuatha mythology. The first battle took place just after the Tuatha Dé Danann first arrived in Ireland. Immediately on arrival, they burnt their ship so that they could not even consider returning or retreating. It was on the plain of Mag Tuired that they met with and slew a hundred thousand of the Fir Bolg. After the battle, it is said that the Fir Bolg fled to the islands of Arran, Mann and Rathlin. Because Nuadu, King of the Tuatha, lost his arm in the battle he had to surrender his kingship. The Tuatha Dé Danann then made a pact with the Formorians under the kingship of Balor, and Bres was elected king. The Formorians were a race of people from the north-western part of Eire. Bres, who was half Formorian and half Tuatha, created great hardship and poverty amongst his people, such that even the human gods were reduced to servility – with the (WHO?) Ogma having to gather his own firewood and the Dagda reduced to digging and building trenches. Bres ruled for seven years, and during that time Nuadu's physician made him a replacement silver arm, which worked better than a real one. Joined by the Dagda, Lugh and Ogma, Nuadu had Bres deposed from the kingship. This event caused a bitter feud between the Formorians and the Tuatha Dé Danann that led to the second battle of Mag Tuired. After much bloodshed, the Tuatha Dé Danann warriors, encouraged by the Morrigan Goddess of War, forced the Formorians into the sea. The Morrigan declared the Tuatha Dé Danann rulers of all Eire.

THE TEN OF WANDS
KEY WORDS

Time to rebalance	*Manipulation*
Burdened by responsibility	*Unreliable*
Overburdened by success	*Immature*

UPRIGHT MEANING: Success does not necessarily bring happiness. It's time to look at how you are managing your time and energies. You may be trying too many things at once, when you should be delegating some of your responsibilities to others. You feel overburdened by the responsibility of being in charge. You feel responsible for your current relationship difficulties and you feel that only your actions can rectify the situation.

REVERSE MEANING: The Ten of Wands in the reversed position suggests that you may be misusing your power to manipulate those around you. Bad decisions lead to bad results, and it is now time to understand how and where you have gone wrong and take steps to rectify matters. You are learning the hard way that there are no easy ways to success.

RELATIONSHIP MEANING: The Ten of Wands suggests that both people in the relationship are prepared to accept the responsibilities of their relationship and are working together to make it successful. In the reversed position, it indicates that one partner is not accepting responsibility for their actions within or outside the relationship and the other partner is feeling very over-burdened by the lack of trustworthiness.

THE STORY OF THE CARD: Oisín had spent many years in Tir Na nÓg and enjoyed every delight there that was to be enjoyed. He had great adventures that would keep a mortal warrior more than happy. But Oisín was, after all, human, and would spend many hours standing on the seashore, gazing longingly across the sea towards his homeland. Even though he had every-thing a man could desire, he finally decided that he must see Eire once again. Niamh pleaded with him not to go back, but when he insisted she made him promise two things – that he would not step off the horse he was riding, and that he would return as soon as he had seen his homeland. Oisín set forth and soon came to Eire, where he made straight away for the famous fortress of the Fianna on the Hill of Allen in Kildare. He was dismayed to find it dilapidated and overgrown. He searched the roads and woods, but found no sign of any of his friends or any members of the Fianna. He thought that much had changed in the short period of time that he had been away. The once familiar buildings were all gone and replaced with dif-ferent types of cottages. Oisín rode among the cottages. The villagers were small, poorly-dressed people, unlike the tall, strong warriors he had known. He rode down a lane where he came across a group of men struggling with a boulder. As he greeted them courteously, he leaned from the saddle to help push away the rock. As he leaned, the saddle girth strained and snapped. Oisín fell to the ground, and as he lay there his hair turned grey and his body began to shrivel up as he turned into an old man. The white steed turned and went back to the Otherworld. 'Who are you?' the villagers asked Oisín as he lay at their feet. 'Oisín of the Fianna, son of Fionn mac Cumhaill,' he answered. 'The Fianna and Fionn are only part of our his-tory now, gone long ago, over 300 years,' they replied. It was only then he realized that he had been away many hundreds of years, and that it was only the magic of Tír-na-nÓg that had kept him young. It is said that in his old age, Oisín was unable to look after himself. Saint Patrick took him in so that he might convert him. However, Oisín left Saint Patrick and went to the plain of Kildare where he had a companion dig up Finn's spear and war horn. From there he made his way to Manorhamilton in County Leitrim, where he died.

THE PRINCESS OF WANDS
Astrological Key: Any combination of Fire elements
Astrological Signs: Aries, Leo, Sagittarius

KEY WORDS

Enthusiasm	*Immaturity*
Dynamism	*Bad temper*
Ambition	*Fickleness*

UPRIGHT MEANING: The card of the Princess of Wands represents an enthusiastic young person who is dynamic and creative; a person who enjoys living for the moment, loves challenge and is often the bearer of good news. It's time to use your creativity and start in a new direction, no matter what your age. Leave things to chance once in a while. Provided you don't take too many risks, everything should be okay. In a career reading, it can indicate the offer of a job or a new opportunity to do with business.

REVERSE MEANING: In reverse, this card suggests someone who has sudden outbursts of bad temper when they cannot get their own way. There is a sense of someone who has an immature attitude. You may suffer from an inability to start new things or it could be that you lack the enthusiasm and energy to follow things through. It can suggest a passionate relationship that will soon burn itself out.

RELATIONSHIP MEANING: The Princess of Wands is impulsive and passionate. She enjoys physical activity, so it is only natural that she will want her partner to share her interest in outdoor activities. She enjoys partying and has no problem leaving one partner for another at a moment's notice if the new person offers a more exciting relationship. The Princess in the reversed position suggests a person who chooses to immerse herself in physical activity to the point that it becomes an obsession.

THE STORY OF THE CARD: Tailtiu, a female fertility symbol, is depicted as an earth goddess and as Goddess of Lughnasadh, which means 'festival of Lugh' – Lugh was the Celtic God of Light. The festival is normally held on 31 July. The wife of Eochu mac Eirc, who was King of Ireland and lived at Tara, Tailtiu was thought to be from Spain, from where she was taken to Eire by Eochu. This tale also credits Eochu with being the father of Lugh the Sun God, and believes him to be the last king of the Fir Bolg. Eochu was killed at the famous battle of Mag Tuired. His death symbolized the end of the Fir Bolg era in Ireland and the start of the rule of the Tuatha Dé Danann. Tailtiu, along with her people, undertook to clear the forest of Coill Cuan, County Meath, in order to create playing fields. It took a year to complete the task. Tailtiu became ill and died while helping to remove a huge oak tree root from the ground. A different version of the story of Lugh tells that Cian was Lugh's father and gave him to Tailtiu to raise as a foster child. Lugh promised Tailtiu on her deathbed that he would hold an annual sports festival of horse racing, feats of battle and other physical challenges in her honour. Lugh held games for a fortnight before and after Lughnasadh (the eve of 1 August) until 1169. In medieval times, trial marriages were held at her sacred burial site, in Telltown, County Meath, to promote fertility. These trial marriages lasted a year and a day and if they did not prove to be fertile could be dissolved.

THE PRINCE OF WANDS

Astrological Sign: Sagittarius
Astrological Influence: Ruled by Jupiter, it is a positive, mutable Fire sign, sometimes tactless, often happy-go-lucky, insincere, impulsive, changeable and selfish.

KEY WORDS

Dynamic energy	*Irrationality*
Unexpected opportunities	*Risk-taker*
Positive, creative movement	*Self-centred*

UPRIGHT MEANING: The Prince of Wands represents a person between the ages of 25 and 40 who is energetic and positive and brings new opportunities, ideas and creative, dynamic energy to a situation. A Fire Sign type, with sandy or reddish hair, this card indicates a person committed to developing his or her abilities. A real go-getter, the Prince inspires others and is a good leader.

REVERSE MEANING: The Prince of Wands suggests a man who revels in conflict or who, because of his desire for immediate action, will sometimes make unnecessary mistakes. He does not always learn from these mistakes, however, and will often make the same errors time and time again.

RELATIONSHIP MEANING: The Prince of Wands generally finds it difficult to stay in one relationship. When in a relationship, he is usually emotionally controlled and a little self-centred. In the reversed position, he is cold and critical and condescending. He likes to use his quick mind verbally to hurt others who are vulnerable.

THE STORY OF THE CARD: Ferdiadh was a warrior of the Domnainn tribe, from north-west Mayo, who trained under Scathach in Scotland. While he was there, Cú Chulainn was placed under his guidance. During their time in Scotland, they became blood brothers and were loyal and true friends. During Medb's raid of Ulster, the Cattle Raid of Cooley, Medb sought revenge on Cú Chulainn because he had rejected her sexual advances. She sent each of her warriors in turn to fight Cú Chulainn. Cú Chulainn killed all of them in single combat. Though the bravest and most fearsome warrior of Connacht, Ferdiadh initially refused to fight his blood brother Cú Chulainn, until finally he succumbed to Medb's insults and agreed to fight him. Each day for three days they fought from dawn to dusk, then embraced and exchanged food and medicinal herbs. On the fourth day, during the fiercest fighting yet, Cú Chulainn killed Ferdiadh using his powerful spear the Gae Bolga. Cú Chulainn carried Ferdiadh to the Ulster side of the river saying, 'Yesterday he was greater than a mountain; today he is less than a shadow.'

THE QUEEN OF WANDS

Astrological Sign: Leo

Astrological Influence: Ruled by the Sun, the centre of the universe, it is a positive, fixed Fire sign, sometimes arrogant, often generous, creative, self-confident, passionate and courageous.

KEY WORDS

Subtle charm	*Jealousy*
Intelligence	*Pride*
Sympathetic character	*Uncaring nature*

UPRIGHT MEANING: The Queen of Wands depicts a woman who has a dynamic energy and a creative approach to life. She loves excitement and challenge in love, and can be spontaneous in passionate situations. She can display an exceptional business sense, loves to be in control and own her own business, life and love. The Queen of Wands describes a woman over 22 years of age, with a vibrant, outgoing nature. She acts on her feelings, is confident and enjoys action. This person attracts many friends and her enthusiastic energy is a pleasure to be around. Nothing gets in her way, and she refuses to be held back by what others see as obstacles. The Queen of Wands believes in her abilities and is generally prepared to take up any challenge that takes her fancy, even at a moment's notice.

REVERSE MEANING: The image of this card reversed is that of a selfish, rest-less, unpredictable and temperamental 'drama queen'. In the reversed position, the Queen is a domineering character who creates conflict for the sake of it. She suppresses her emotions and becomes problematic in relationships. The Queen reversed can also indicate a woman who has lost hope – she is unable to see her way out of a particular relationship or situation.

RELATIONSHIP MEANING: Always encouraging her partner to bigger and better things, the Queen loves excitement and positive emotional interaction. She has a magnetism that attracts many offers of love. She takes great care in whom she chooses as a long-term partner, though she will sample many before making her final decision. In the reversed position, this Queen becomes domineering and demanding. If ignored by others, she becomes more demanding and tends to drain the energy from those around her.

THE STORY OF THE CARD: Macha was the daughter of Aed Ruad. She became the wife of Cimbaeth, King of Ireland and founder of the Red Branch Knights, who lived at Emain Macha, which is now known as the Navan Fort. One tale tells that Macha's father Aed Ruad shared the kingship of Ulster with his cousins, Dithorba and Cimbaeth. The kingship was rotated between them, and this system worked for over 45 years until Aed Ruad drowned in an accident. Macha assumed her father's position when the time came for his turn. Dithorba and Cimbaeth would not agree to her becoming Queen and a battle ensued. Macha won the battle, married Cimbaeth and together they ruled Ulster. Cimbaeth was planning to build a new fort. He knew of Macha's special divining powers, and so he requested that she choose the best place for him to build this new stead. Using all her skills and wizardry, she divined the most secure design and position, and not long after it was built their magnificent ring-fort became the ruling centre of Ulster, and later the royal court of Ireland. Cimbaeth named the fort in honour of Macha. Another tale tells that, a long time later, Macha fell in love with Cruind, a farmer connected to the ring-fort. She went to his house and, after circling three times outside the front door, she entered his house and made love with him in his bed. She became pregnant. A few months later, Cruind boasts to Cimbaeth that Macha could race any horse and win. Despite Macha's plea of pregnancy, Cimbaeth demanded that she run the race against his fastest horse. After crossing the winning line, she gave birth to twins, but lost her own life. With her last breath she cursed Ulstermen for nine generations.

THE KING OF WANDS
Astrological Sign: Aries
Astrological Influence: Ruled by Mars, the planet of war, Aries is a positive, cardinal Fire sign, sometimes self-centred, often fiery, energetic, assertive and lacking staying power.

KEY WORDS

Influence	*Aggressive*
Conscientiousness	*Ruthlessness*
Dynamic energy	*Macho behaviour and violence*

UPRIGHT MEANING: The King of Wands has strong principles; he inspires confidence with his skilfulness and his ability to get things done. The King of Wands is the card of a person with a dynamic, creative energy. His maturity and wisdom can be of great assistance to those under his care, and he is a good leader. He has a great dislike for routine, loves constant challenge and is a great initiator of new ideas, but sometimes finds it hard to follow them through to their conclusion. He is generally great fun to be with, and has a good sense of humour.

REVERSE MEANING: In the reversed position, the King of Wands has similar qualities to those in the upright meaning, except he has a softer nature, or has not yet fully matured. He may lack the drive and commitment to follow his ideas through to their completion.

RELATIONSHIP MEANING: The King of Wands tends to be sexually aggressive and likes to collect beautiful partners as trophies. When in a permanent relationship, he may try to restrict his partner by use of verbal aggression.

His lovemaking always contains a degree of dominance. In the reverse position, he may be violent and intolerant to the attitudes of his partner, with a tendency towards egocentricity and ruthlessness.

THE STORY OF THE CARD: Conchobar mac Nessa became King of Ulster by default in the first century BC. At this time, Fergus mac Roich was King of Ulster and wished to marry Ness, mother of Conchobar mac Nessa. She agreed on one condition – that her son be made king for a year. While in power, Conchobar was a fair and just king, and was well liked by both warriors and chiefs. When the year was up, Conchobar refused to return the throne to Fergus. The Red Branch Knights, an army of highly trained warriors, constantly protected Conchobar and he used this army to drive Fergus into exile. When Conchobar was wounded in a battle with cattle raiders, his physician warned him that because of the damage to his head he should always remain relaxed and never become angry. It is said that he lived for 70 years, but eventually died in a fit of rage, on hearing of the birth of Christ.

THE ACE OF CUPS
KEY WORDS

New Beginnings	*Fatigue*
Happiness	*Loneliness*
Abundance	*Disappointment*

UPRIGHT MEANING: The Ace of Cups represents a new beginning, a rush of joy at the beginning of a new project, partnership or relationship. This is the beginning of a period of fulfilment or the start of something new, which gives you enjoyment, pleasure and joy. It suggests that this new opportunity has the potential to be built upon and developed, so that it continues to bring fulfilment and happiness in the future.

REVERSE MEANING: When the Ace is reversed, it can suggest unhappiness due to an emotional, disruptive situation. There is a feeling of stagnation in emotions; or it may be a sense of loss or failure in a partnership, situation or issue. It can represent despair or a loss of faith in someone. A situation has arisen that has led to a time of unhappiness for you. The Ace reversed can also suggest that you may have been let down – maybe false promises have been made by a friend, or someone has broken a promise to do something that was very important to you.

RELATIONSHIP MEANING: This card indicates the start of, or potential for starting, a new relationship. It can also indicate that you are moving into a frame of mind where you are open to the possibilities of taking on a new relationship, even though previously your attitude was closed or you were not ready to take on a new relationship. This is a time for expressing your true feelings and emotions. There may be a regeneration of love in a present relationship. The cards surrounding the Ace of Cups will give you more clarity as to which of these options is more realistic.

THE STORY OF THE CARD: The suit of Cups corresponds to the element of water, the ruler of emotions and feelings – love, hate, jealousy, happiness and sorrow. The Cup in the illustration is that of the Ardagh Chalice – the cup of enlightenment, representative of the Holy Grail. Sought for so long by so many, it was believed that taking one sip from the Holy Grail would bring 'all knowledge' or complete enlightenment, the union with the Divine. The Dagda, or 'Good God', one of the gods of the Tuatha Dé Danann and keeper of the Cauldron of Abundance, was associated with the Holy Grail in Arthurian legend. The Dagda returned from the Otherworld with the Cauldron of Abundance, which could feed all and leave no one hungry. The Ace of Cups, like all Aces, can be seen as a gift from the gods, the gift of an opportunity. It sits glowing in the window, and beyond the window is a bright, optimistic future – only you can choose to take it or leave it.

THE TWO OF CUPS
KEY WORDS

Love	*Emptiness*
Understanding	*Misunderstanding*
Balanced partnership	*Incompatible partnership*

UPRIGHT MEANING: The Two of Cups indicates the start of a relationship or partnership that is trusted. It is the start of a business partnership in which the people involved have a mutual understanding of the commitment involved. And they also understand each other's expectations. This card suggests a project which is in its infancy, but which has the potential to grow and become successful. It can indicate the forming of a partnership with another person or people that has great potential. It also represents the beginning of a very special relationship between two people.

REVERSE MEANING: In reverse, the Two of Cups suggests a disagreement or the cessation of a partnership due to incompatible expectations. It is time to take the first step to resolve a disagreement or argument. Don't let something small grow into an issue that cannot be resolved.

RELATIONSHIP MEANING: This relationship is at a very early stage. The two people involved have so much to offer each other, to build on for the future. It may be the time for the first pledging of love to each other for the present and also for the future. This is the time to let the foundation of love grow into something special. In the reversed position, it indicates emotionally charged quarrels, painful separation, and the loss of trust in a relationship.

THE STORY OF THE CARD: Grainne, the daughter of King Cormac, is promised against her will to Fionn mac Cumhaill. At the wedding feast, Grainne, who is in love with the handsome Diarmuid, administers a sleeping potion to the whole gathering – with the exception of Diarmuid and three of his friends. She reminds Diarmuid of his *geis* never to refuse a woman in need, and insists that he take her away from Fionn. Diarmuid at first refuses, not wanting to cross his old friend Fionn, but Grainne begins to call down the power of the *geis*, which is destruction and death. Before she finishes speaking, Diarmuid agrees, knowing that to break a *geis* would also bring disgrace to his family. Diarmuid and Grainne become fugitives and so begins one of the greatest love stories in Celtic mythology. They are constantly pursued by Fionn and the Fianna, and have many close encounters with the fearsome warriors. However, each time Diarmuid manages to outwit and overcome the Fianna. For a long time they travel throughout Ireland, living in the forests and at times with friends. For a long time they sleep together, but to Grainne's dismay they do not consummate their relationship. One day as they walk together by a stream, a splash of water lands on Grainne's leg. She tells Diarmuid, 'You are a brave warrior in battle, but this splash of water is more daring than you are with me.' Diarmuid realizes how much he loves Grainne and makes a commitment to her. Shortly after, they marry and celebrate their relationship as shown in the Three of Cups.

The Three of Cups

Key Words

Celebration	*Unhappiness*
Friendship	*Promiscuity*
New lifestyle	*Lack of commitment*

UPRIGHT MEANING: The Three of Cups shows a celebration of a partnership; it suggests that the first stage of a plan has been achieved successfully and the people involved are making a commitment to the future. In a career or business question, it represents good fortune or preliminary success in the early stages of a business relationship.

REVERSE MEANING: In the reversed position, the Three of Cups represents failure of a partnership or a business that does not come up to your expectations. It can also warn that you should be careful when making long-term plans, as one of the people in the partnership may not be ready to make a long-term commitment. This card can also suggest abuse of substances such as alcohol or narcotics. You may be filled with a sense of hedonism, with too much partying and perhaps not taking enough responsibility.

RELATIONSHIP MEANING: The card can also represent different kinds of celebration, like an engagement, a wedding or pregnancy, or the birth of a child. It suggests two people moving their relationship on to the next stage, possibly moving in to live together – a feeling of initial completion. The Three of Cups can stand for a mood or experience that makes you feel like dancing and singing. In the reversed position, it indicates that circumstances within a relationship have changed. It augurs the failure of a relationship because one of the people involved may not be ready to make a long-term commitment.

THE STORY OF THE CARD: While on the run from Fionn and the Fianna, Diarmuid and Grainne had many adventures. At one point, they came to the land of the One-Eyed Giant, where Diarmuid obtained permission to hunt on the giant's territory, provided they did not touch the berries on the giant's magic tree. One day, passing the magic tree, Grainne, now seven months pregnant, was overcome with a longing for the ripe, plump, juicy red berries and quickly snatched one from the tree. The angry giant jumped down from his tree-house and threatened to kill her. Diarmuid took the giant on in a combat that lasted half a day before he finally slew the giant. The fugitive couple moved into the giant's tree-house, but shortly after the Fianna surrounded them. Aengus, one of the Fianna, offered them both protection and a home at his palace in Meath. Diarmuid insisted that Grainne go with Aengus, and promised to meet them there if he survived the challenge of combat with the other members of the Fianna. Diarmuid won the combat and followed Aengus and Grainne to Meath. They remained in Aengus' protection until, after 16 years of tireless negotiation, Aengus secured an amnesty from Fionn for Diarmuid. Cormac mac Airt was pleased to be able to forgive his daughter and Diarmuid for eloping. Diarmuid was then granted his dead father's land and possessions, free from tax and tribute.

THE FOUR OF CUPS
KEY WORDS

Boredom	*Renewed vigour*
Lack of motivation	*New ideas*
Procrastination	*Involvement*

UPRIGHT MEANING: The Four of Cups indicates that having achieved certain goals, you no longer find pleasure in the success. It can suggest that you have grown weary of day-to-day activities, discontent on an emotional level. And there is a lack of motivation to take on new challenges and achieve high goals. On the surface you may seem happy, yet there is unhappiness within, a situation that is stagnant. When this card is drawn in a reading, it suggests that you may have lost interest in your current situation, and it's time to look for new interests and challenges. Others may be trying to instil doubt into a relationship or situation.

REVERSE MEANING: You are aware that the time for reflection is over and action is now required. New opportunities are waiting. You must actively seek them out for they will not be where you think they are. You should be taking the time to think through emotional issues.

RELATIONSHIP MEANING: In a relationship reading, the Four of Cups suggests that one or both people may have lost interest in working on the relationship and have been looking to a new person or other interests for fulfilment. On the surface all may seem happy, yet you have a suspicion that something is just not right. You have an empty feeling inside and a knowledge that the relationship has come to a standstill. It is time to work at either bringing new excitement or passion to the current relationship or seeking out a new passion altogether.

THE STORY OF THE CARD: The Wooing of Étain is an important tale of the Mythological Cycle. Midir was invited by the Mac Óc to stay for a year as a guest. He was rewarded with a chariot and a maiden whose beauty and gentleness surpassed that of all the maidens in Ireland. She was Étain Echraide, daughter of Ailill, King of Ulster. At the end of the year, Midir returned with Étain to his own land at Brí Leith. His wife Fuamnach became jealous and asked the Druid Bresal to put a spell on Étain. Bresal's spell caused Étain to turn into a butterfly. However, Midir recognized her and she stayed with him for many years until Fuamnach discovered her. Fuamnach had her cast to the wind for seven years. She landed on the shoulder of the Mac Óc who built a sun bower for her. When Fuamnach heard that Étain was with the Mac Óc, she cast her to the wind again. Many years later, Étain arrived at the court of King Conchobar mac Nessa. She fell into Étar's wife's golden tumbler, and was reborn nine months later as Étain, daughter of Étar. At that time, Eochaid the King of Ireland was looking for a wife. Hearing about the beautiful Étain, he had her brought to him and married her. Midir heard of this union and went to the Hill of Tara where the King lived. By magic Midir disguised himself and challenged the King to a game of chess, the prize being one kiss from the new

Queen. Midir won the game and claimed his prize. As Midir kissed Étain, he wrapped his arms around her and by magic they rose into the air and flew away, never to be seen again.

THE FIVE OF CUPS
KEY WORDS

Empty relationship	*Reunion*
Loneliness	*Unexpected gift*
Rejection	*Inheritance*

UPRIGHT MEANING: This card brings with it a sense of loss, sorrow, emotional emptiness or a sense of rejection in a relationship. However, it also tells us that all is not lost in this relationship. Four of the five cups may be spilt, but one still stands, suggesting that no matter how hopeless things seem, there is always something to be saved from a situation. Sometimes we don't know the value of something until we come close to losing it. This relationship has not yet completed its journey so all hope is not yet lost. Take care not to spend too much time feeling sorry for yourself – it is more important to hold on to the cup that is still standing than to cry over the four that are spilt.

REVERSE MEANING: You are ready to move on and release yourself from the past, to forgive and to forget. You now accept that what's done is done, and you know that the pain will go if you are prepared to let it go now. Its suggests that it's time to you to stand alone and not to place too much trust in anyone or anything for the present.

RELATIONSHIP MEANING: The Five of Cups indicates a sense of loss within a relationship, and perhaps a feeling of emotional emptiness. You think that you are being rejected by someone you love, yet this card tell us that all is not lost. One of the five cups is standing, indicating that there is still something in this relationship to be worked on. In the reversed position, it suggests the redevelopment of a relationship after a break-up.

THE STORY OF THE CARD: Ess Euchen was a powerful female magician whose three sons were killed by Cú Chulainn. Ess Euchen chose to believe that Cú Chulainn was totally responsible for the death of her three sons, failing to understand that her sons had any part in provoking Cú Chulainn into a combat with them. Though her friends tried to help her deal with her despair and grief, she decided to seek revenge. Through magic she found out that Cú Chulainn would be passing close to were she lived. So she turned herself into an old crone and waited along a dangerous, narrow, mountain path for Cú Chulainn. As he came close, she stepped out and demanded that he move aside to let her pass. Her intention was that as Cú Chulainn moved aside, she would push him off the cliff edge to his death. However, sensing evil from the old woman, Cú Chulainn used the magic leap that Scathach taught him when he was training in Scotland and jumped over her. As he passed over Ess Euchen, she pushed out to try and reach for him, but slipped off the cliff and fell to her death.

THE SIX OF CUPS
KEY WORDS

Pleasant memories	*Contention*
Nostalgia	*Being found out*
Serenity	*Arrogance*

UPRIGHT MEANING: It is now a time of looking back and reliving pleasant times of the past. From the past will come happiness. It may come in the form of an old friend or a surprise. Take time out to enjoy the good moments, for they are very special. This card also indicates it is a time for making new friends and laying solid foundations for the future. There is a sense of generosity concerning feelings, nurturing and caring.

REVERSE MEANING: In the reversed position, the Six of Cups can indicate the act of moving from a secure situation in search of stimulation and challenge. Perhaps you are moving from home, or leaving a secure job for a more challenging, risky career.

RELATIONSHIP MEANING: The Six of Cups suggests contentment within a relationship. This relationship is one that is based on a common understanding and commitment to each other. Two people are working towards the same goals. In the reversed position, it indicates a relationship that is open to experiment and new experiences and open to interaction.

THE STORY OF THE CARD: Findabair and Froach look back on their lives and the joy they have found from being together. They have suffered many tribulations and Froach has nearly lost his life, but for them it has been worth all the pain and they are serene in the knowledge that they were meant to be together. Findabair was the daughter of Queen Medb and King Ailill of Connacht. Medb and Ailill wanted Findabair to marry the champion warrior Ferdiadh. However, Findabair had other ideas as she was in love with Froach. Famous for her courage and conviction, and believing a woman should make her own decisions, she went ahead and made known her decision to wed Froach without permission from her parents. Medb planned Froach's demise and insisted that before he marry Findabair, he must swim in the lake of the dragon monster. As soon as the dragon attacked him, Findabair rushed to save him and together they slew the monster. Froach was badly injured in the fight, but a number of the fairy folk helped nurse him back to full health. Medb and Ailill eventually gave in to Findabair's wishes and she married Froach with their consent.

THE SEVEN OF CUPS
KEY WORDS

Problems	*Determination*
Possibilities	*Commitment*
Choice	*Positive attitude*

UPRIGHT MEANING: There is a sense of illusion, of living in a fantasy world, that comes with this card. The Seven of Cups indicates it is a time to sit back and identify honestly your needs. You may be fooling yourself. You need to be candid with yourself – stop looking for perfection in everything. You will only end up disappointed and feeling let down. Better to be a little practical and concentrate on everyday life, because if you don't you may find that as you spend your time in your dream world, imagining how everything should be, real life will be passing you by.

REVERSE MEANING: The Seven in reverse can indicate that you are being too practical in your approach to your relationship or work. It is necessary to be practical, but you should also make time for your human side. You may be locked into collecting all the material things in life. However, there is more to life than things, and you risk missing out on this.

RELATIONSHIP MEANING: You may feel that something is missing within your relationship, but you can't identify exactly what it is. It is time to look at what is on offer in your relationship and see if your needs are being met, but it is also time to look at what you are putting into your relationship. There is a great need for honesty and candour, and you need to stop dreaming of an ideal world. You would do yourself more good by concentrating on the real world and identify what you need to do to improve it, rather than just imagining how things would be in a perfect world.

THE STORY OF THE CARD: Connla, son of Conn of the Hundred Battles, was out hunting near the Hill of Uisneach. This place marked the exact centre of Ireland. A beautiful damsel approached him, and invited him to go with her and live forever in Mag Mell, one of the names for the Otherworld. He refused, but as she departed she left him an apple upon which he lived for a month without any diminution of its size. Shortly after the month was up, Connla was walking by the lake when a boat pulled up beside him. Once again the maiden approached him. This time, she wove images of Mag Mell around him, painting a picture of a place where everything is bountiful, young and beautiful. She told him that Mag Mell was a place without pain or suffering, where there was freedom from fear and death and all the people lived peaceful and happy existences. She talked of a place in which there was no one save women and maidens. Connla decided to go with her, jumped onto the boat and started to row away to this wondrous land. However, it was only while they moved away from the land of Eire that he stopped for a moment as he realized that he would never again see his friends or his native land, because once a mortal visits the Otherworld, returning to the human world brings instant death.

THE EIGHT OF CUPS
KEY WORDS

Moving on	*Material pleasure*
Change of plan	*Problems*
Abandoning a path	*The unknown*

UPRIGHT MEANING: This card carries a feeling of loss of energy or tiredness. You may feel like abandoning a relationship, or taking a complete change of direction in your career. You feel that you are not on the right path and there is no point in trying to continue in that direction. It's time to choose a new direction. You are tired of the way things are. It may be time to move away from a relationship that is not going anywhere. You realize that you may have taken a wrong turn in the search for fulfilment. It is now time to move on from a stagnant situation.

REVERSE MEANING: You are feeling negative at the moment. There is a loss of direction and you have no sense of which path to take next. You are reluctant to leave a situation or relationship, even though you know that there is nothing left there for you. You may be pretending that you're happy in an unhappy situation.

RELATIONSHIP MEANING: You may have unrealistic expectations of your partner or relationship; perhaps a sense of fantasy or illusion. It may be that this relationship exists entirely in your imagination. In the reversed position, the card suggests a powerful desire to pursue a person and develop a relationship. There is an overwhelming sense of love for someone, and this person may not be reciprocating these feelings.

THE STORY OF THE CARD: Iseult, daughter of an Irish king, was promised in marriage to King Mark of Cornwall. King Mark asked his nephew Tristan to go to Ireland to escort Iseult back to Cornwall. Iseult was unhappy about this marriage and did not want to leave Ireland. Iseult's mother was a powerful magician and because she was concerned that Iseult would be unhappy in her marriage, she gave Isolde's lady-in-waiting a love potion. This was to be given to the couple on their wedding night, to ensure a love match between Mark and Iseult. During the voyage to Cornwall, Iseult and Tristan accidentally drank the love potion and they fell completely in love. When they arrived in Cornwall, Iseult was forced to keep her word and marry King Mark, but she continued to meet Tristan in secret. King Mark finally found out about their secret love and Tristan was forced to flee to Brittany. He married Iseult of the White Hand, but it was a marriage in name only. One day, in battle, he received a fatal wound from a poison arrow. He immediately called for his real love Iseult of Ireland, with a message that if she came to him aboard the returning ship, it was to fly a white flag. If she were not on board, it would show a black flag. When news of the approaching ship reached Tristan, his jealous wife told him that the flag was black. He died of a broken heart, moments before his true love, Iseult of Ireland, reached him. When she saw his dead body, she collapsed and died of grief alongside him. They were buried together, and the two trees that grew over their graves intertwined.

THE NINE OF CUPS
The Wish Card

KEY WORDS

Much happiness	*Limited rewards*
Success	*Limited view*
Accomplishment	*Being deprived*

UPRIGHT MEANING: Often called the 'Wish Card', the Nine of Cups suggests fulfilment having overcome difficulties. Your efforts will be rewarded. It indicates the celebration of a relationship or a feeling of emotional contentment within a relationship – honest love gained through a deep commitment between two people. You may find yourself receiving a lot of positive attention, feeling and being appreciated by others.

REVERSE MEANING: In the reversed position, the Nine of Cups indicates self-centredness – a selfish need for or an addiction to pleasure or fulfilment on a basic level. You may be accused of wanting to receive much more than you are prepared to give. It can also suggest an addictive personality, with addiction to drugs, alcohol, food or sex.

RELATIONSHIP MEANING: This card suggests emotional balance and harmony within a relationship. This is a relationship that provides security and support for the needs of each of the partners involved. In the reversed position, it suggests there is a lack of emotional harmony within a relationship. It may be that the relationship restricts one or both partners in finding fulfilment.

THE STORY OF THE CARD: Caolainn was a local deity and the guardian or queen of a magical well in County Roscommon, in the west of Ireland. She was known for her gift of granting wishes. Often she granted these wishes to people in order to show them that they did not really want or need the things they wished for. One story tells of the time when Caolainn met a young man who was smitten by her beauty. He spoke in rapturous tones of the whiteness of her skin, the blackness of her hair, which nearly reached the ground, and the blueness of her eyes, which were the colour of corn-flowers. He wished that his beloved had these eyes, which were full of light and magic. Without a word, Caolainn plucked them out and, with warm blood dripping from them, threw her beautiful eyes at the stunned young man. 'Be careful what you wish for,' she told him, 'for you may just get it!'

THE TEN OF CUPS

KEY WORDS

Celebration	*Heartache*
Contentment	*Disagreement*
True love	*Thoughtless actions*

UPRIGHT MEANING: The Ten of Cups represents a relationship that has reached a genuine state of ongoing contentment. You are now reaping the rewards of your efforts. There may be a wedding or some other celebration of love and happiness, some kind of outward show of a relationship in which both people are totally committed to each other in love and trust. There is a feeling of trust, commitment and contentment with the other person.
REVERSE MEANING: In the reversed position, the Ten of Cups indicates a relationship or family situation where the people are detached from each other on an emotional level. In a career situation, it suggests a group of people who are not working well together and, if this situation is allowed to continue, eventually there will disagreements and a break-up of the partnership.
RELATIONSHIP MEANING: The Ten of Cups in a relationship reading suggests that you are now reaping the rewards for the efforts you have made in the past. Your relationship environment is stable, happiness is forecast. Honesty, love and trust abound in a satisfying family life.
THE STORY OF THE CARD: It was a warm summer's day as Fionn and his son Oisín, along with other members of the Fianna, were out hunting by the

banks of Loch Lein. Coming towards them, they saw a beautiful woman on a white charger. Her golden hair danced in the wind as she rode in their direction. She was wearing a white robe with a flowing purple cloak; her brooch and jewellery were of the heaviest gold, and on her head was a crown of gold encrusted with precious stones and gems. 'My name is Niamh of the Golden Hair. I am the daughter of the King of Tír-na-nÓg , and have come to invite Oisín to be with me in the land of the Ever Young.' Oisín, a romantic and a poet of high standing, fell instantly in love with her. He had heard tales of this fruitful and beautiful land, and could not resist this vision of beauty. Fionn pleaded with his son, warning him that if he went with Niamh he could never return to the land of Eire, or his family and friends. However, Oisín was overcome by his love for the beautiful stranger, and he agreed to go with her. A sadness fell over the group as Oisín and Fionn bade each other farewell and Oisín mounted the white horse behind Niamh. In the blink of an eye, they were gone from sight and soon they were flying high above the clouds. Oisín looked down on the waves of the sea as the land of Eire faded away into the distance and felt a momentary sadness. But he lived happily with Niamh for many years in Tír-na-nÓg.

THE PRINCESS OF CUPS

Astrological Key: Any combination of water influences
Astrological Signs: Cancer, Scorpio, Pisces

KEY WORDS

Good news	*Fastidious*
A dreamer	*Possessive*
Emotional understanding	*Jealous*

UPRIGHT MEANING: A loving message is on its way. The Princess of Cups can represent the opportunity of a new relationship or partnership. This card can also suggest the development of a present relationship to a deeper emotional level. Reflective and caring, the Princess of Cups offers a deep understanding of emotional issues. Her message is love moving to a deeper level. It can indicate a person who has a youthful attitude to life and a balanced understanding of emotions. It may suggest the arrival of good news or news to do with the birth of a child.

REVERSE MEANING: In the reversed position, the Princess of Cups indicates a person who is immature and selfish and will take advantage of an emotional situation for his or her own gain. This may be a person of emotional immaturity who seems to swing from one mood to the next, not considering the feelings of those around.

RELATIONSHIP MEANING: The Princess of Cups in a relationship has an emotional depth that only a partner with equal depth could understand. She tends to be full of feeling, but can be prone to moodiness and clinging. She is sometimes jealous and obsessive. The princess in the reverse position suggests a person who lives in a fantasy world.

THE STORY OF THE CARD: Eri of the Golden Hair was a virgin goddess of the Tuatha Dé Danann. She was walking by the bank of a river in a thoughtful and reflective mood when a man in a silver boat glided to the bank beside her. He was surrounded by a beam of sunlight so powerful that Eri was overcome with emotion. She joined him on the boat and they made love. His name was Elther and he prophesied that she would have a son. He gave her a ring and told her to put the ring on her son's finger, when he was man enough to wear it. Nine months later, she gave birth to a son, who was called Bres. Bres became King of the Tuatha Dé Danann and High King of Ireland. However, he only ruled for seven years. It is said that because of his lack of generosity and compassion the poet Cairbre made him an object of satire 'until boils appeared on his face'. Bres then had to resign his kingship because only those who were physically perfect were permitted to rule Ireland.

THE PRINCE OF CUPS

Astrological Sign: Pisces
Astrological Influence: Ruled by Neptune, the planet of illusion. It is a
negative, mutable Water sign, sometimes self-effacing, often dreamy,
imaginative, artistic and compassionate.

KEY WORDS

Elusive lovers	*Possessive partners*
Emotional interaction	*Addicted to emotions*
Creative activity	*Self-serving*

UPRIGHT MEANING: The Prince of Cups suggests a focusing on creative, artistic abilities. The Prince of Cups can indicate an offer from someone in their twenties or early thirties, or someone with the emotional attitude of this age group. This card suggests a person who is enthusiastic and open to new ideas. As with all the cards of Cups, this person has a good understanding of their emotions and is probably offering the opportunity of a new relationship, or wants to develop a relationship to a deeper level. There may be an offer of engagement or marriage.

REVERSE MEANING: The Prince of Cups reversed shows an immature, easy-going person – a charming 'flirt' – someone who is not taking a relationship seriously. The Prince reversed also offers a warning about someone who is making an offer for all the wrong reasons. It may be that they want to develop a relationship for monetary gain rather than for love; or it may be someone who wants to marry as a means to something else – perhaps a visa for entry into another country.

RELATIONSHIP MEANING: Love is the food of life for this Prince, and he is constantly on the look-out for someone new who may have the potential to bring more emotional fulfilment than the present partner currently does. When the first flush of love wears off, he often becomes bored and quickly loses interest. In the reversed position, the Prince can become addicted to his emotions. When this happens, the rest of his life can suffer to the point that he can lose his job or let his career fall by the wayside.

THE STORY OF THE CARD: Cú Chulainn, warrior to the High King, met and fell in love with Emer, daughter of Forgall Manach (Forgall the Wily). Forgall did not want Emer to marry Cú Chulainn, so he entered into secret negotiations with the High King. The High King called for Cú Chulainn and told him that he was being sent away to Scotland to train with the famous female warrior teacher Scathach the Shadowy One. Forgall hoped that, in his absence, Cú Chulainn would forget about Emer, or that Forgall would be able to persuade her to marry someone else before Cú Chulainn's return. Before Cú Chulainn left for Scotland, he and Emer made a promise to wait for each other, no matter how long they were to be apart. After spending many years away, Cú Chulainn returned to Forgall's fort and they both realized that their love was as strong as ever. Against Forgall's wishes, Emer and Cú Chulainn decided to leave and marry. They went to live at Cú Chulainn's stronghold, where they were not separated until Cú Chulainn's death.

THE QUEEN OF CUPS
Astrological Sign: Scorpio
Astrological Influence: Ruled by Pluto, the transformer, it is a negative, fixed Water sign, sometimes inflexible, often dynamic, intense, dominant and sensual.

KEY WORDS

Understanding	*Over-sensitive*
Sensitive	*Sentimentality*
Intuitive	*Inconsistency*

UPRIGHT MEANING: The Queen of Cups has a loving and sensitive nature. She is gentle and kind and has a deep understanding of emotional issues.

Guided by her feelings, she gives good, honest advice, but you may not always like the advice she gives, because you know it to be the truth. Touch is an important part of her healing process, and she loves to embrace. When in a crisis situation, her healing energies are tangible, even at a distance.

REVERSE MEANING: There are two types of Queen of Cups in the reversed position. The first suggests a woman who is prone to depression or is becoming despondent when she loses hope. If things take a turn for the worst, she sometimes finds it hard to grasp any sense of hope for the future. The second image of the Queen of Cups reversed suggests a vain, flirtatious woman who takes rejection very personally. However, if the Queen of Cups is rebuffed, she becomes vindictive and seeks revenge for the deep sense of rejection she feels.

RELATIONSHIP MEANING: The Queen of Cups is often dependent on others for emotional fulfilment. She is strong and clear in her objectives, and these are mainly focused towards a strong, loving relationship and family environment. She sometimes lives in a world of romance and fantasy. Unfortunately, due to her over-vivid imagination, the Queen of Cups is often attracted to the wrong type of partner – the sultry, dangerous, impulsive type. She knows in her heart that he is not the right type of partner for her, but she thinks that she can change him and make him into the type of man she needs. However, he is the type who will eventually bring her world tumbling down.

THE STORY OF THE CARD: Áine was a sun and fire goddess, who was sometimes called Áine of Knockainey. She was strongly identified with midsummer, with growth, potential and development. She destroyed Ailill Olum, the King of Munster, with her powerful magic because he raped her. She made a vow that she would never fall in love with a grey-haired man. She became infatuated with the young warrior Fionn mac Cumhaill, and Fionn showed similar interest in her. Áine's sister, Miluchrach, became very jealous because she was in love with Fionn. Áine had told Miluchrach of the vow she had made, and Miluchrach decided to take advantage of it. Miluchrach gathered her friends together and cast a magic spell on a lake close to home. One day soon after, Fionn was out hunting deer with his hounds when he came across a beautiful lady crying by the lakeside. She pleaded with Fionn to recover her lost ring from the lake. Fionn dived into the lake and recovered the ring. But when he surfaced, the lady was gone and Fionn had turned into an old man, so old that even his hounds did not recognize him. Finally, the other warriors of the Fianna found him. Fionn, who had known of Miluchrach's jealousy, figured that she was responsible for the spell on him. For three days, Fionn and his warriors held the fairy mound of Sliabh Guilleann under siege until Miluchrach admitted she had been responsible for turning him into an old man. Her father was furious and insisted that she give Fionn a magic potion that allowed him to recover his youth. The potion worked, but with one exception and that was that his hair stayed grey. Áine kept her vow and refused any further advances from Fionn.

THE KING OF CUPS

Astrological Sign: Cancer
Astrological Influence: Ruled by the Moon, it is a negative, cardinal
Water sign, sometimes moody, often emotional, insecure, intuitive,
responsive and protective.

KEY WORDS

Hidden strength	*Sensitive*
Wise	*Easily manipulated*
Diplomacy	*Flatterer*

UPRIGHT MEANING: The King of Cups is wise and understanding with a deep knowledge of the world. He is also a caring, sincere individual who responds to the need of others. He is a good counsellor, a healer who stays calm under pressure. Others turn to him for advice because they know his intuition is second to none. The guidance he gives will, if followed, offer the correct path to take. He is tolerant of views that are different from his own and is not easily shocked. This person moves forward carefully, considering each move he has to make.

REVERSE MEANING: This King in the reversed position represents a man who is weak-willed and wants to dominate relationships. Because of his lack of self-esteem, he may be involved in a number of relationships, constantly seeking assurance and acceptance from others, instead of seeking self-knowledge. He is sometimes tortured by the pain of the failure of past relationships or from his childhood.

RELATIONSHIP MEANING: Generous and attentive, the King of Cups feels happiest in a relationship when he can be the benefactor and provide security. He is genuinely interested in the feelings of others, and quickly backs away from people who are emotionally cool. In the reversed position, it suggests a person who manipulates others by taking advantage of the other person's emotional insecurity.

THE STORY OF THE CARD: Niall of the Nine Hostages became King of Ireland in AD 379. One day, while out hunting, Niall and his stepbrothers went to draw water from a well in a forest when a cailleach (an old hag) stopped them. She told them that there was a *geis* or curse on the users of the well. The *geis* was that whoever wanted to use the well had to kiss her. The other young men stared at the wrinkled, grey-haired old hag in front of them and recoiled in horror. However, Niall embraced and kissed her as passionately as if she were a goddess. Just as he did, she turned from an ugly old crone into a beautiful woman. Niall asked her who she was. She told him she was Sovereignty and that Niall would be 'King of Ireland one day and his blood line would be in every clan of Ireland'. Her prophecy came true. Niall ruled for 27 years until he was assassinated on the banks of the River Loire in France by one of his Clan Chiefs.

The Ace of Swords
Key Words

Clarity	*Confusion*
Movement	*Stagnation*
New ideas	*Violent action*

UPRIGHT MEANING: The Ace of Swords represents power, clarity and movement, which can be used for either good or evil. It also indicates clarity of thought and the ability to instigate change and bring about positive movement in the right direction. There is a new beginning: by having a clear purpose you can achieve what you desire. This card suggests the awakening of mental energies, which initially may create conflict, but ultimately will lead to growth and development.

REVERSE MEANING: The Ace of Swords represents clarity of thought – it is double-edged, suggesting the ability to see both sides of a situation. Now is the time to be careful of the changes that are being made. These changes could be negative or damaging to you or others. You sometimes find yourself wanting to make changes just for the sake of change, with no idea of what direction you want to go. This generally indicates that you will expend a lot of energy and actually achieve nothing.

RELATIONSHIP MEANING: In a relationship reading, the Ace of Swords indicates that you have a new-found confidence in yourself and in your ability to establish a relationship. In the past, there may have been opportunities to establish a new relationship, but because of a lack of faith or confidence in yourself you did not take them. In the reversed position, it indicates that you may be refusing to take no for an answer; or refusing to hear the truth behind someone else's refusal.

THE STORY OF THE CARD: Nuadu Argatlam or Nuadu of the Silver Arm was King of the Tuatha Dé Danann for seven years before they came to Eire.

Nuadu lost his arm during the first battle of Mag Tuired in which the Tuatha Dé Danann beat the Fir Bolg, some of the original settlers of Eire. Brehon law stated that a king had to be completely able-bodied, and so Nuadu was disqualified from the kingship. The Tuatha Dé Danann went into council to appoint a new king. An agreement was reached that Nuadu's cousin Bres, the son of the Formorian King Elatha, would rule the Tuatha Dé Danann. Bres in turn would marry Brigit, the daughter of the Tuatha Dé Danann god The Dagda. Bres oppressed his subjects with excessive taxes, tyranny and avarice and brought great hardship on the people of Eire. It took a full seven years for Nuadu's physician Dian Cécht to make him an artificial arm of silver. But so skilfully was the arm made that all the joints moved, even those of the fingers. It was at this time that the Tuatha Dé Danann, no longer able to tolerate his tyranny, called upon Bres to abdicate and asked Nuadu, who was now able-bodied, to take the throne again. During a feast held at Tara, the capital of the Tuatha Dé Danann, to celebrate his return to the throne, Lugh appeared, ready to aid in the forthcoming battle with the Formorians. For the Formorians, furious that Bres had been deposed as King of the Tuatha Dé Danann, had declared war upon them.

THE TWO OF SWORDS
KEY WORDS

Delicate balance	*Deceit*
Indecision	*Misrepresentation*
Conforming	*Resentment*

UPRIGHT MEANING: It is now the right time to make a decision, yet there is a sense of being caught between a rock and a hard place. You are torn by indecision; you are unsure whether or not you are ready to face certain issues that need to be faced. You may also feel you have reached an impasse and do not know which way you should proceed.

REVERSE MEANING: In reverse, the Two of Swords warns you to be on your guard against misleading information. It can suggest that you are afraid to face the truth, or are making excuses as to why you should not deal with issues that need to be dealt with. There is no point procrastinating, you know that certain issues need to be sorted out so that you can move forward.

RELATIONSHIP MEANING: The Two of Swords suggests that you are uncertain about a relationship or relationship situation and do not know how to deal with it. It can also indicate that there is no love in your relationship, yet you fear facing up to the problems within this situation. This may be because you are afraid of being alone. In the reversed position, the Two of Swords suggests a relationship built on lies and deception, which will not bring good to anyone involved.

THE STORY OF THE CARD: One of the saddest tales of Celtic mythology is that of Deirdre of Sorrows. Conor mac Nessa, King of Ulster, had attended a feast in his honour in the home of Feidlimid, his bard. It was late, the feasting was over and everyone was settled down for the night. Feidlimid's wife, who was heavy with child, was slowly making her way to her own quarters when the child in her womb gave a shriek so loud that it woke all the guests in the house. The Druid Cathbad was called in for an interpretation of the meaning of this terrible cry. Cathbad pronounced, 'This child will be a girl, and will grow to be the most beautiful woman in all of the land. She will be called Deirdre and because of her beauty there will be great sorrow, and her grave will be a lonely mound, and her story will be told forever.' The King commanded that when she was born, she was to be banished to the far end of the kingdom. True to Cathbad's word, she was called Deirdre and grew up to be the most beautiful woman in Ireland. As a young woman, she started to have strong dreams of a beautiful young warrior named Naoise. Naoise was one of three brothers. He met Deirdre some time later and they both fell instantly in love. However, Deirdre was so beautiful that at the same time Conor, who was the King of Ulster, became infatuated with her. He ignored the predictions of Cathbad and made many proposals of marriage to her. Angered at her refusal, he set out to kill Naoise. Deirdre and Naoise escaped to Scotland, but once again, Deirdre's beauty worked against her and a Scottish king began to pursue her. With no other option they had to return to Eire. Through her dreams, Deirdre knew that no matter where they went, pain and sorrow would follow them. When Conor heard that the couple had returned, he had Naoise and his brothers ambushed and killed. When Deirdre was being taken to the royal court on the back of a wagon, she realized she could not live with the loss of Naoise. The wagon sped towards the royal court and, as they approached a tree with heavy, overhanging branches, Deirdre stood, closed her eyes and called out her lover's name as the branches of the tree knocked her from the wagon, killing her instantly.

THE THREE OF SWORDS
KEY WORDS

Separation   *Loss of direction*
Pain   *Errors*
Strife   *Self-delusion*

UPRIGHT MEANING: The Tree of Swords indicates pain and suffering as a result of your actions. There is a feeling that you would have done things in a different way if you had had the chance again. The Three can also indicate divorce, separation, or the break-up of a relationship or partnership. This card also tells us that the tide is turning, and things can only get better.

REVERSE MEANING: In the reversed position, the Three of Swords has a similar meaning to that in the upright position, except that you may be denying or suppressing your feelings. It is now time to face up to the truth of your situation and take positive action to deal with the issues that need to be dealt with. This card offers optimism once you start dealing with your situation.

RELATIONSHIP MEANING: This card indicates pain and suffering within a relationship. Separation and loss are great pains to bear and there is an overwhelming sense of emptiness for a period of time. Sometimes we have to experience this sadness and pain before we can move on. In the reversed position, the Three of Swords suggests that you are not prepared to let go of a violent or incompatible relationship.

THE STORY OF THE CARD: Here we meet Aífe, a fearless warrior, who was the sister of Scathach. Scathach was the female warrior who ran a warrior school in Scotland where Cú Chulainn was sent for training. While Cú Chulainn was there, there was trouble between Aífe and Scathach and Cú Chulainn had to go into single combat with Aífe. Knowing that Aífe was impervious to magic, Cú Chulainn used deceit to win the combat. They fell in love and she became his mistress. Before Cú Chulainn left Scotland, he gave Aífe a gold ring; Aífe told him that she would bear him a son and pleaded with him not to leave. However, Cú Chulainn returned to Ireland and married Emer. Aífe had a son, whom she named Conlai. She was determined to seek revenge, so she trained Conlai to be a powerful warrior. She placed Conlai under three *geasa:* he could not give his name when asked, he could not stand aside for anyone he met on his path, and he could not refuse to fight anyone. Aífe was sure that Conlai would kill Cú Chulainn in combat and sent him to present himself at his father's court. However, Cú Chulainn killed Conlai in combat. It was only when he saw the gold ring on Conlai's finger, that Cú Chulainn realized he had killed his own son.

THE FOUR OF SWORDS
KEY WORDS

Tread carefully　　　　　　　　*Loneliness*

Meditation　　　　　　　　*Disaster*

Be aware　　　　　　　　*Need for action*

UPRIGHT MEANING: It is time to pull back and take a look at your situation from a cool, calm and collected position. Even though you may want to focus and take action on one issue, it is important that you look at the greater picture and take all things into consideration before making important decisions. You may soon be facing a change of lifestyle, moving yourself into a more settled way of living.

REVERSE MEANING: The four in reversed position can indicate a speedy recovery from illness. It is now the right time to get back into the routine of everyday life. It is time to put into action the new lessons learned from your past experience.

RELATIONSHIP MEANING: This card indicates in a relationship reading that there is a need to step back and become a little less involved. Take time out to look at exactly what your emotional needs are. Re-evaluate your relationship and see if it fulfils your needs. It does not mean that your relationship is over, but that you may need a temporary break from it.

THE STORY OF THE CARD: Bricriu of the Evil Tongue was simply a troublemaker and was known and avoided because of it. He had a talent for and took great pleasure in stirring up trouble. Bricriu built a palace at Dun Rudraige, equal in size to that of the Red Branch Knights at Emain Macha, but he made sure it surpassed Emain Macha in splendour. He held a feast for Conor mac Nessa, and invited all of the principal warriors and their wives. Conor was honour bound to attend any feast held for him. Because of their distrust of Bricriu and his ability to create mischief, King Conor and the other chiefs only agreed to go to the feast on the condition that Bricriu left the room before the feast began. Bricriu agreed, and ordered his cooks to prepare a magnificent cauldron, only to include the choicest cuts of meat. It was tradition that the champion warrior would receive the champion's portion. As his guests arrived, Bricriu wasted no time in setting the seeds of trouble in the minds of his guests by whispering to a number of the warriors that they should claim the champion's portion. When Bricriu was leaving the hall before the feast, he turned to his guests and said in a loud voice: 'The champion's portion is over there, make sure only the champion gets it.' Three charioteers rose to claim it for their masters as instructed earlier by Bricriu. 'Bring it over here to the champion!' shouted Laeg, Cú Chulainn's charioteer. Immediately, the other warriors sprang to their feet, drawing their weapons. Conor pleaded with the chiefs to calm their men and not give in to the trickery of Bricriu. The others recognized the trickery and allowed the portions to be divided equally between the champion warriors.

THE FIVE OF SWORDS
KEY WORDS

Loss	*Dishonour*
Conflict	*Indecision*
Separation	*Malice*

UPRIGHT MEANING: This card suggests disagreement and conflict. You may have won the battle, but much has been lost. There may be a separation under difficult circumstances. It should be remembered that a stubborn, strong-willed attitude will not resolve an issue. The Five of Swords can often indicate the break-up of a partnership under adverse circumstances. Now is the time to swallow your pride and accept the inevitable.

REVERSE MEANING: The Five of Swords reversed indicates disagreement and separation, where those involved are more inclined to be open to discussion. You need to look beneath the surface for the real truth. If involved in a business or legal matter, ensure that you check out the small print, as it is here that the real truth of the matter lies.

RELATIONSHIP MEANING: In a relationship, the Five of Swords suggests trouble and strife. One of the partners in this relationship is deliberately manipulating the other. He or she has consciously or subconsciously taken on board an attitude, which will be completely destructive to the relationship. In the reversed position, the card suggests guilt or anxiety about your behaviour; you are discovering your mistakes when it is too late

THE STORY OF THE CARD: Fionnula and her three brothers were the children of Llyr and Aebh. After Aebh's death, Llyr married Áife, who was so jealous of Llyr's love for his children that she put them under a spell, turning them into swans and condemning them to a life of hardship and pain. The spell lasted for 900 years. They were bound to spend 300 years on Lough Derravaragh, 300 years on the Sea of Moyle and 300 on the Atlantic Ocean. They spent these years in cold, miserable conditions. To try and help her brothers survive the spell, Fionnula taught them to sing, and the sorrow in their voices was so haunting that people came from the length and breadth of Ireland to hear them. Towards the end of the 900 years, they found sanctuary with a hermit monk on the island of Inis Glóire. Lairgren, the King of Connacht, sent a messenger to the island to bring the swans to his court as a present for his new bride. The messenger chained the four swans together, but before he got to his boat to return to the mainland, the 900 years came to an end. The swans turned into four old people lying helpless on the ground. In a soft voice, Fionnula asked the hermit to baptise them and bury them on the island. The children of Llyr died peacefully together with the holy hermit praying over them.

THE SIX OF SWORDS
KEY WORDS

Hard work pays off   *Powerless*
Success after trouble   *Harassment*
Moving out of troubled waters   *Delays in travel*

UPRIGHT MEANING: You are now moving your life out of turbulent waters into calm waters, towards achieving your goals and aspirations. There may be more challenges ahead, but you are over the worst. You are now leaving a difficult situation. Your difficulties are nearly over.

REVERSE MEANING: Having succeeded in overcoming some obstacles, you now face even more. Your journey is far from over, but you may need to rest before proceeding. You have committed yourself to a course of action, and you must follow it through to the end.

RELATIONSHIP MEANING: You have successfully overcome some difficult relationship problems, and have moved your relationship to a new, positive level of understanding. But let things rest for a while before you attempt to deal with the next set of issues that need to be dealt with.

THE STORY OF THE CARD: At one point during Cú Chulainn's stay in Scotland, he met Aífe, a beautiful princess who had no equal in battle and whose beauty was matchless. Some tales tell us that Aífe was Scathach's sister. She was not vulnerable to magic, and commanded a legion of fierce female warriors who fought on huge horses. Aífe was hated by the very jealous Scathach, Cú Chulainn's martial arts tutor. Scathach thought the time was right to wage war on Aífe. As Cú Chulainn was Scathach's best student, Scathach told only him about the power of the deadly Gae Bolga, which was to play such an important part in Cú Chulainn's future and in the history of Eire. Aífe's warriors were brave but matched by Cú Chulainn, who inspired Scathach's warriors to daring deeds. Seeing her warriors slaughtered, Aífe challenged Scathach to single combat. Cú Chulainn, fearing for Scathach, offered to fight on her behalf. First, he asked Scathach what were the things most valued by Aífe. Her two horses, her chariot and her charioteer,' Scathach replied. Cú Chulainn was awestruck by Aífe's beauty but strongly challenged by the fierceness of her combat. Cú Chulainn and Aífe used all their skills as champion warriors against each other. But all in vain, until a mighty blow by Aífe shattered Cú Chulainn's sword to the hilt. The power of the blow sent Cú Chulainn to the ground. As Aífe moved in for the kill, Cú Chulainn shouted, 'Your horses and chariot are falling into the abyss!' In alarm, Aífe glanced around and in that instant, Cú Chulainn grabbed her and slung her over his shoulder and bore her back to Scathach's camp. Aífe begged for her life as Cú Chulainn held a knife to her throat. Cú Chulainn told her that he would spare her life on one condition – that she and Scathach should make lasting peace with each other.

THE SEVEN OF SWORDS
KEY WORDS

Defeat	*Self-deceit*
Dishonesty	*Deceit*
Hidden motives	*Frustration*

UPRIGHT MEANING: You may need to use guile to achieve success, as a direct confrontation would be disastrous. If you have no choice but to confront your enemy, then choose your time and place carefully. Find your enemy's weak point and disarm him in advance. Underhand behaviour may be going on behind your back – manipulation, vicious rumours.

REVERSE MEANING: There is little reward for your present effort, and you may need to change your plans. Let go of outmoded attitudes and ideas. You are fooling yourself and now need to change your way of thinking. Lots of talk and no action means no results. You feel that you have been given unreliable advice, or that there is a lack of support for your efforts.

RELATIONSHIP MEANING: You are taking a detached approach to your relationship, and may be guilty of clever manipulation of your partner. You may see your partner or relationship as a means of achieving your own personal goals, or as a way of gaining recognition from others.

THE STORY OF THE CARD: One of the Three Sorrowful Tales of Erin tells of how the sons of Tuirenn slew Cain, father of the Sun God Lugh. This was an old feud and Cian was always aware that he was in danger. Cian was in the Boyne Valley in preparation for the battle of Mag Tuired when he saw three armed brothers approaching. Realizing he was outnumbered, he used his magic wand to change himself into a pig and joined a nearby herd of pigs. Brian, one of the brothers, spotted the magic cloud made by the change, but his brothers Iuchair and Iucharba did not. So Brian changed his two brothers into hounds, setting them on the pigs. When the magic pig was separated from the herd, Brian speared it. The brothers turned back into human form and when they realized what had happened, they asked Brian to spare Cian's life, but Brian refused. Cian asked to be allowed to turn back into human form before death, and Brian granted this request before he finally killed Cian. Old Irish or Brehon laws did not demand the death sentence for taking a life, but imposed a price to be paid called a blood fine. Because it was Lugh's father who had been killed, the Druids placed a very heavy fine on the three brothers. This involved a number of gigantic challenges, which would place their lives very much at risk if they were to fulfil the payment of the fine. These challenges included obtaining the magic 'Spear of Assal' belonging to the King of Persia, bringing back three apples from the Garden of Hesperides, getting a chariot and two horses from the King of Sicily and giving three shouts from the Miodchaoin Hill in Lochlainn. They succeeded in all their tasks until the last when Miodchaoin challenged them and Brian killed him. Miodchaoin's sons followed the sons of Tuirenn and seriously wounded them, but they managed to return home. On their arrival, they pleaded with Lugh to allow them to be healed by magic, but he refused and they died.

THE EIGHT OF SWORDS

KEY WORDS

Major difficulties

Restrictions

Isolation

Depression

Little reward

Desperation

UPRIGHT MEANING: Bound by the difficulties around you, you feel restricted and powerless. In your past, you have handed over your power to someone else or to circumstantial control. You have to dig deep and find the inner strength to allow you to free yourself from your present position.

REVERSE MEANING: You are now free to see things as they really are. You have the ability to make decisions for all the right reasons. Old beliefs and attitudes that have restricted you can be replaced with a new, clearer understanding on some or all levels.

RELATIONSHIP MEANING: The Eight of Swords indicates that you feel powerless within a relationship. You have handed over your power to your partner. You may have a fear of leaving an empty relationship in case you don't find someone else.

THE STORY OF THE CARD: Sionnan was the granddaughter of Manann mac Lir the Sea God. She went to the sacred well of the Cailleach to perform a ritual. She had total disrespect for the correct ritual and had not prepared properly for it. She had not yet learnt the importance of the old ways, and refused to consider the great powers she was going against. The gods were angry at her disrespectful attitude to the sacred well, for this was no ordinary well; it was the great well of knowledge. They placed a high price on her sacrilege. Enraged by the lack of respect, the sacred waters of the well rose up and pulled her under, carrying her from the life she knew to another, foreign existence. They later abandoned her on the banks of the Shannon River. It is said that she spent hundreds of years, roaming from one fairy mound to another, seeking entry to the Otherworld. Refused at every entry entrance, she is now believed to be found rambling along the banks of the Shannon River.

THE NINE OF SWORDS

Nightmares	*Subconscious answers*
Worry	*Prophetic dreams*
Sleeping difficulties	*New, positive attitude*

UPRIGHT MEANING: Negative thoughts, worries and concerns are overwhelming. You may find yourself subject to sleepless nights or nightmares due to a feeling of pain and despair. It can also indicate bereavement or the loss of something that you value deeply. You have a tendency to put yourself down without justification.

REVERSE MEANING: The Nine of Swords reversed indicates that you are now likely to face your fears, confront your old lack of ability or self-esteem and take positive action to make changes on new terms. If there is a problem with an addiction of some kind, the Nine suggests that you are now ready to face this addiction, and hopefully break your habit.

RELATIONSHIP MEANING: In a relationship reading, the Nine of Swords can suggest a relationship empty of emotion. It can also indicate that you fear that your relationship will break up. This fear is probably without foundation, but you are consumed by worry.

THE STORY OF THE CARD: Suibne Geilt was a chief of the clan Dal nAraide. It is said that Suibne Geilt went mad because of a spell that the Druids who supported his enemy, King Domnall, had put on him. They determined that he be 'cursed by the bells and crosiers of clerics' – in other words, the sound of church bells and the sight of monks' crosiers would drive him crazy. At the battle of Mag Rath, it happened that Suibne finally lost his reason. He jumped onto the shield of a warrior who was fighting and then up into a tree. The elders watching the battle were dismayed to see their King acting in such a strange way. He stayed in that state in the tree until a shower of hail stones fell. He then disappeared from sight into the wilderness, moving from tree to tree, and living only on water and watercress. After many years of wandering, Suibne settled at Tech Moling in Carlow.

Taking pity on Suibne, Moling told his cook Muirgil to give him some milk each day. Muirgil's husband became jealous of the attention his wife was paying to Suibne. One day, as Suibne sat drinking the milk that Muirgil had brought him, Muirgil's husband went into a rage and threw a spear at Suibne. The spear entered Suibne's left breast and split his backbone in two, killing him instantly.

THE TEN OF SWORDS
KEY WORDS

Ruin	*Disgrace*
Failure	*Suffering*
Disaster	*Violence*

UPRIGHT MEANING: This card indicates that you feel that you are being mistreated in some way; you are either being abused verbally, or someone may be stealing from you. The Ten of Swords can often represent the total end of a situation or relationship, or the collapse of a business. You may have in some way brought yourself to this point by mismanagement or attitudes that were out of touch with the reality of the situation. It is time to surrender and allow necessary change to take place.

REVERSE MEANING: In reverse, the Ten of Swords suggests a situation of violence, suffering and pain, or an unforeseen calamity of your own making or of the making of others. You have the ability to remove yourself from this situation, but it will take great strength and character.

RELATIONSHIP MEANING: You feel that you cannot go on after a relationship has ended. You are suffering from anxiety and worry about the future of a relationship. Or you may be suffering in silence about the loss or death of a partner. There is a sense of depression and the feeling that you cannot go on, or that there will be nobody there for you in the future.

THE STORY OF THE CARD: Bres became King after the battle of Mag Tuired, in which the reigning King Nuadu lost his arm in combat. The law of the land dictated that only a man who was physically perfect could hold the kingship, so Nuadu was forced to step down and hand the kingship of Ireland to Bres. Bres forced tributes from the human gods of the Tuatha Dé Danann, Dagda, Ogma and Lugh. During this time, he married Brigit, a daughter of the Dagda. This intermarriage between the Tuatha Dé Danann and the Formorians was a way of keeping peace. Bres demanded excessive tributes from all and created much hardship for his people until the Druid Cairbre decided that something had to be done. He met with the poet Cairbre to see how they could usurp Bres without warfare. Cairbre was a Druid poet with special powers and great wit. He made Bres the subject of his satire. Cairbre's poetry was so powerful and had such an effect on Bres that boils and carbuncles began to appear on his face. Bres called on many different powers to try and remove these ugly blemishes from his face. But Cairbre's power was too strong. The boils and carbuncles became so unsightly that eventually Bres was forced to resign his position in the same way that he gained it.

THE PRINCESS OF SWORDS
Astrological Key: Any Air Sign influence
Astrological Signs: Gemini, Libra, Aquarius

KEY WORDS

Inspiration	*Indecision*
Good news	*Lack of action*
Mental activity	*Inactivity*

UPRIGHT MEANING: This card suggests the arrival of a letter, or news that will mentally challenge you. The Princess represents a mentally active and highly skilled person who stimulates new ideas and thoughts. Though not always grounded in reality, the Princess can act as a catalyst and give inspiration to others who can take these ideas and develop them in a more practical way. In a relationship reading, the Princess of Swords suggests that you have a dreamy attitude to love and romance.

REVERSE MEANING: In the reversed position, it suggests that you are daydreaming or fantasizing rather than trying to put your ideas into action. This card in reverse can also represent a stubborn person who often creates disagreements just for the sake of it.

RELATIONSHIP MEANING: In a relationship reading, this Princess tends to be hard to please, seeming to be unhappy, and she probably is. It is not that she is unhappy in this particular relationship – more that she tends to be unhappy anyway, always seeing the negative rather than the positive. In the reversed position, the Princess can become self-absorbed in her concepts and ideas in which everyone must take part, if only for a peaceful environment. If you question her ideas, she can become contrary and disgruntled.

THE STORY OF THE CARD: Uathach, a goddess who trained warriors to fight, assisted her mother Scathach at the warrior school in Scotland. The first woman Cú Chulainn met on his journey to train under Scathach was the daughter of Donall Dornalla, or Donal of the Big Fist, who fell in love with him. She was furious when Cú Chulainn rejected her love, but Cú Chulainn ignored her cries of revenge and continued on his journey. On the final leg of the journey, Cú Chulainn came to the Bridge of the Cliff. There he met Uathach, who told him that he must perform one act of valour before he could cross the bridge. He immediately performed the Hero's salmon leap and jumped across the bridge without touching it, landing at the feet of Scathach. One day during training, Cú Chulainn accidentally broke Uathach's finger. Her lover Cochar Crufe heard her screams and challenged Cú Chulainn to fight because of this insult to his woman. Cú Chulainn killed Cochar and as a fine, Scathach made Cú Chulainn take over Cochar's position as guardian of the island for a year and a day. Cú Chulainn and Uathach became lovers.

THE PRINCE OF SWORDS

Astrological Sign: Gemini
Astrological Influence: Ruled by Mercury, the planet of communication.
It is a positive, mutable Air sign, sometimes inconsistent, often shallow,
volatile and extrovert.

KEY WORDS

Clever	*Devious*
Shrewd	*Complex*
Skilful talker	*Economical with the truth*

UPRIGHT MEANING: The Prince of Swords indicates a man who is active and committed to developing his ideas to their full potential. It usually represents a young man with a quick mind, who is coming into your life to offer something; it may be love, an idea or an object of some kind. Because this person thrives on activity, he will leave in a flash if you take too long to consider his offer.

REVERSE MEANING: The Prince in reversed position is usually a warning about someone who is devious and underhand. This man is careless, impatient and extravagant, and will take over a situation. He may seem very convincing, but will be liable to let everything fall apart through lack of action.

RELATIONSHIP MEANING: This Prince is determined to have his way, whether or not you want him in your life. While being very charming, he tends to be controlling and is very clever in how he manipulates things to make sure he gets his own way. In the reversed position, the Prince of Swords is known for compiling information to be used for his own advantage at a later date. He is disruptive and will take advantage of any weakness shown by others.

THE STORY OF THE CARD: Loegaire was the son of Niall of the Nine Hostages, and he became King of Ireland around AD 430. He ruled for 30 years. During this time, Saint Patrick was admitted into Loegaire's court and, before long, had converted Loegaire to Christianity. Sometime later,

Loegaire attacked the fort of King Lagin, demanding outstanding payments and royalties. Loegaire's army was quickly defeated at the battle of Athdara, and Lagin demanded that Loegaire make a promise that he would never again demand a *bórama* or attack the people or property of Lagin. Loegaire agreed and made the following promise: 'By the sun and moon, day and night, water and air, sea and land, I will never again demand a *bórama* from Lagin.' It was prophesied that he would die between Eire and Alba (Ireland and Scotland) and so he swore never to travel by sea. A number of years later, having rebuilt his army, Loegaire once again planned to attack Lagin. He decided that he could outwit the prophecy. On his way to battle, he was passing through a valley between two hills called Eire and Alba. Suddenly, a howling wind swept down from the hills and lifted him from his horse into the air where the sun burnt him to death for breaking his promise.

THE QUEEN OF SWORDS
Astrological Sign: Aquarius
Astrological Influence: Ruled by Uranus, the planet of discovery. It is a positive Air sign, sometimes rebellious, often opinionated, detached, loyal and tolerant.

KEY WORDS

Solitary	*Devious*
Independent	*Dominant*
Secretive	*Cold*

UPRIGHT MEANING: The Queen of Swords represents a woman who is rational and logical, with a well-functioning mind. This person has definite ideas as to how things should be done; she is shrewd and mentally agile. She has a careful approach to relationships and is attracted by mental agility rather than looks. She does not give her heart freely in love, and has a penetrating mind. She is confident and capable of turning a situation to her best advantage. She is a woman who may isolate herself due to disappointments in her past.

REVERSE MEANING: In the reversed position, the Queen of Swords gives a serious warning – be aware of someone near you who is unhappy, and delights in seeing others unhappy too. She likes to stir up trouble, tends to be cold-hearted, shrewd and very manipulative. You are not likely to suspect this person of causing trouble, but she is very capable of making others as unhappy as she is herself .

RELATIONSHIP MEANING: In a relationship, this Queen is a mentally strong partner and seeks out her partners not for love or looks, but for their own mental agility. She does not suffer fools gladly. This woman has the ability to hide the emotional side of her nature – often to the point of showing no emotion in any situation. In the reversed position, she is cold by nature, very sharp and not to be crossed at any price.

THE STORY OF THE CARD: Queen Medb (Maeve), regarded as the historical Queen of Connacht, was probably the most famous of all the Queens in Celtic mythology. Her name means 'intoxicated woman' and she was known as the 'Goddess of War' because of her fiery temperament and her aggressive attitude to battle. Medb appears in many of the most famous tales of Irish Celtic Mythology. Described as a beautiful, long-faced woman with long, flowing hair, and believed to have reigned at the beginning of the Christian era, Medb was the daughter of Eochaid Fedlech, King of Tara. She had two sisters – Clothru, Queen of Connacht, and Eithne. Medb killed Clothru, who was pregnant with the child of Conor mac Messa. The child was saved 'when it was taken out of her side with swords'. Medb, along with her husband Ailill, immediately took over as rulers of Connacht. Medb was a most sensuous and earthy queen and was known to have many lovers. It is said that 'she replaced one man in the shadow of another', but most of all she desired the warrior Cú Chulain. Medb ruled with an iron fist and showed little mercy for anyone who crossed her. There was only one restriction that Medb voluntarily observed and that was the *geis* she was under to bathe in a spring every morning at the end of Inis Clothrand on the River Shannon. It was here that Clothru's son Furbaide killed Medb to avenge his mother's death.

THE KING OF SWORDS
Astrological Sign: Libra
Astrological Influence: Ruled by Venus, the planet of love. It is a positive, cardinal Air sign, sometimes prevaricating, often indecisive, dogmatic, supportive and light-hearted.

KEY WORDS

Leadership	*Dominance*
Intelligence	*Cunning*
Balance	*Deceitfulness*

UPRIGHT MEANING: This man likes to get his own way, and will use his mental prowess to do so. He is a clear-thinking man who uses his mental abilities to pursue his goals. He is generally innovative in creating change, and is capable of pursuing many different goals at one time. The King is an achiever, who takes great care when developing plans and makes sure that others follow his directions to the letter. He always has a clear understanding of what is happening around him and manipulates others to get his own way.

REVERSE MEANING: The King of Swords reversed often suggests a man who requires others to match him step by step in mental arguments or discussions, otherwise he will always get his own way. If this card is in an influential position, you must take care not to be bullied, pushed or persuaded against your better judgement.

RELATIONSHIP MEANING: This King has an intellectual, quick mind and a sharp tongue, and derives pleasure from making others look foolish. He loves to challenge others to stand up for themselves, and if they fail the first test, they seldom get a second chance. Love seldom dominates the King of Sword's life, as he is a talker rather than a doer. In the reversed position, the King of Swords can be a troublemaker, and is emotionally cold and cruel at the best of times.

THE STORY OF THE CARD: Conn Cét Chathach (Conn of the Hundred Battles) was a famous High King of Ireland. He lived a varied and colourful life until he was just 100 years of age, an extreme age in those violent times of battle and siege. As a result of the battle of Mag Aga, Ireland was divided in two between Conn and Eoghan Mór, who was the King of Munster. Later, Conn was to defeat Eoghan Mór at the battle of Mag Lena, after which he became High King of Ireland. Another tale tells that when Conn was High King, he was out hunting one day when he was surrounded by a magic mist and Lugh the Sun God appeared before him. Lugh foretold to Conn all the kings who were to succeed him. A stone head of Conn was discovered in a passage-grave, showing Conn as the God of Enlightenment.

THE ACE OF PENTACLES
KEY WORDS

New beginnings   *Fatigue*
New emotions in love   *Loneliness*
Abundance   *Disappointment*

UPRIGHT MEANING: The Ace of Pentacles represents the dawning of a new period of realization and prosperity. There may be new beginnings. Not only from a financial perspective, this card can represent a whole new start covering all aspects of your life. You may be starting a new business. This not only has the potential for financial success but will also create success in all other areas of your life.

REVERSE MEANING: The Ace of Swords in the reversed position indicates that a new beginning or idea, which initially seems to have great potential, could prove illusory. Failure and disappointment may follow on the heels of initial success. It may suggest that you are suffering from fatigue following the failure of a relationship or an idea failing to come to fruition. You need to take time out to gather your resources and rebuild your confidence before you start again.

RELATIONSHIP MEANING: In a relationship reading, the Ace of Pentacles indicates that you have a new-found confidence in yourself and in your ability to establish a relationship. You see a new relationship having the potential to develop into what you always desired your future would bring. In the reversed position, you may not see the potential a new relationship has.

THE STORY OF THE CARD: In this illustration, we see the Ace of Pentacles standing on the Newgrange Stone, which is at the entrance to the Newgrange passage-grave. The Newgrange Stone, like the Ace of Pentacles, is representative of new beginnings, growth and development. Newgrange is one of the finest European passage-tombs. The single spiral pattern seen on the stone is the oldest and most recorded motif. It has symbolized the concept of growth, expansion and cosmic energy. For the ancient inhabitants of Ireland, the spiral was used to represent their sun. A loosely-wound, anti-clockwise spiral represented the large summer sun. The dual-centred spiral is also prolific in stone carvings. It has associations with motifs from other cultures such as the Chinese Yin Yang symbol. It signifies the duality of nature and balance. The early Christian monks used triple-centred spirals in their illuminated manuscripts. The motif depicts a trinity of spirals emanating from a single source and may well have been used by the monks to represent the Holy Trinity. Chevrons resembling arrowheads used by hunters and warriors alike were a symbol of power among the Celts. The most famous of all Irish prehistoric monuments, Newgrange was originally built about 3100 BC and has been very well restored. It consists of a vast stone and turf mound, containing a passage leading to a burial chamber. Outside the base, 12 of the original estimated 38 large boulders can still be seen.

THE TWO OF PENTACLES
KEY WORDS

Balance	*Inconsistency*
Knowledgeable manipulation	*Dismissing warnings*
Stimulating developments	*Stagnation*

UPRIGHT MEANING: The Two of Pentacles indicates movement and change in the natural progress of a project or business. You need to decide between two alternatives, as you cannot do both at the one time. One has to be given preference over the other. In a partnership reading, it suggests the need to make a decision based on financial or long-term considerations.

REVERSE MEANING: In reverse, the Two indicates missed opportunities due to your having placed too much emphasis on the pleasures of life. You may not want to admit it, but you now need help from someone else to sort out your financial matters. You may find that you are suffering from an inability to do anything with an opportunity when it comes along.

RELATIONSHIP MEANING: The Two of Pentacles suggests that a relationship will only develop if there is financial security in the present and potential in the future. It can also indicate the opportunity to develop a relationship in a work environment. In the reversed position, it can suggest that one partner may be not be revealing financial difficulties that have come up in the relationship.

THE STORY OF THE CARD: The image of the Two of Pentacles portrays Ogma, one of the three champions of the Tuatha Dé Danann. Ogma, along with the other champions, Lugh and the Dagda, pursued the Formorians to recover the Dagda's magical harp and Ogma's sword. Ogma personified the combination of warrior and orator. He was also known as the Honeytongued, because of his eloquence. He combined magnificent warrior skills with a brilliant mind. It is believed that he invented Ogam, a form of writing, which he handed over to the Druids and which was mainly used for magical purposes. The letters are represented by parallel strokes along a vertical line, originally inscribed in stone, but sometimes etched on tree bark and branches as secret messages and warnings for other Druids. The Ogam alphabet consists of 20 letters and five diphthongs, with the letters grouped in fives, probably indicating a relationship to the five fingers, allowing finger signs to be used as a means of passing secret messages to each other. Ogam inscriptions have been found on hundreds of large and small stones, on the walls of some caves, and also on bone, ivory, bronze and silver objects.

THE THREE OF PENTACLES
KEY WORDS

Material gain	*Conflicts*
Craftsmanship	*Incompatible motives*
Joint action	*Wasted opportunities*

UPRIGHT MEANING: This card suggests that the first stage of a project or business has been achieved successfully and the people involved are making a commitment to the future. You must now consolidate your position and ready yourself for the next stage or series of challenges. It can also suggest two people moving their relationship on to the next stage; perhaps where they now have enough money to pay a deposit on a house or apartment. In a career or business question, it represents good fortune or preliminary success in the early stages of a business relationship.

REVERSE MEANING: In reverse, the Three of Pentacles describes a situation that is stagnant and has not advanced or changed for quite some time. It may be that you have not taken advantage of the opportunities that are there now or in the recent past. Reversed in a relationship reading, it suggests disagreements, or a lack of direction or conflict of interests.

RELATIONSHIP MEANING: In a relationship reading, the Three depicts partners who are supportive of each other's ambitions or careers, with an equal desire for financial security. It may represent partners in a relationship who are planning to go into business together. In the reversed position, it suggests conflicts over expenditure or bad spending habits.

THE STORY OF THE CARD: Fionn and his warriors were hunting in Corn in Northern Connacht. Much to the annoyance of the local Danann lord, Conaran, they had not had the courtesy to ask for permission to hunt on his land. He sent his daughters, who were sorceresses, to take vengeance. Fionn and his men were moving slowly along the edge of the Hill of Keshcorran when they came upon three hideous hags who were twisting yarn in a left-hand direction on holly sticks in a cave. Upon investigating, Fionn and Conan became entangled in the yarn, and all those who followed were knocked unconscious and captured, except for one warrior, Oscar, who was Fionn's grandson. He managed to escape. Oscar eventually came to the camp of Goll mac Morna, leader of the second clan of the Fianna. Although Fionn and Goll had the same allegiance and had fought together on the side of the Fianna, they had a great dislike for each other, based on an old family feud. However, Goll agreed to help. He went to the cave and fought ferociously. He hacked two of the hags to death and subdued the third, Irnan. She promised to release the Fianna and his men in return for her own life. As they were catching their breath, the hag attacked again, but Goll killed her immediately. Fionn and Goll agreed to work together for the greater good of the Fianna. Fionn offered the hand of his youngest daughter, Caoimhe, in marriage to Goll as a reward for saving him and his men from the evil daughters of Conaran. Unfortunately, as you will see in the story of the Four of Pentacles, this agreement was not to last for long.

The Four of Pentacles
Key Words

Financial stability *Reluctance*
Development *Clinging*
Expansion *Static*

UPRIGHT MEANING: Power, achievement and control can be gained by overcoming your present obstacles. To do this you need to take control of your spending. You can now move towards financial stability by living within your means. This card can also suggest jealousy and possessiveness, depending on the surrounding cards.

REVERSE MEANING: In the reversed position, it suggests that you are trying to take too much control of a situation for fear of change. Fear of losing control can create a negative or stagnant situation. Too much bureaucracy also creates a stagnant situation.

RELATIONSHIP MEANING: The Four of Pentacles suggests continued interaction and support, with a common focus on increasing financial security and comfort. In the reversed position, the Four suggests either financial overspending by one of the partners within the relationship, or an overinvestment by one of them in the relationship, to the detriment of their own well-being.

THE STORY OF THE CARD: This is the story of a blood feud that occurred between Fionn mac Cumhaill and his arch-enemy, Goll mac Morna. The origin of the hatred went back to the death of Fionn's father at the hands of Goll. Fionn held a huge feast to which he invited all the clans of the Fianna. There were hundreds of warriors at the feast, including Goll mac Morna along with 50 of his tribe. At the end of the feast, Goll demanded *bórama* from his host for lands that he owned. Fionn refused to pay him, as he had already paid by giving him a thousand warriors. Goll was not happy with this and, in retaliation, began to boast of how he had killed Fionn's father in order to acquire these lands. Fionn was overcome with rage and a long and bloody battle ensued between Clanna Baoiscne (Fionn's tribe) and Clanna Morna (Goll's tribe). It took all the mediatory skills of Feargus Finnbhéil, the poet of the Fianna, to separate Goll and Fionn, calm them down and stop the fighting.

THE FIVE OF PENTACLES
KEY WORDS

Financial Troubles	*Courage*
Poverty	*Hope*
Loneliness	*Freedom*

UPRIGHT MEANING: The five of Pentacles augurs a time of financial troubles, poverty and loneliness. It can indicate the loss of a job, or loss of money, which may or may not have serious consequences. It can also indicate loneliness in a relationship. You have a sense of being alone, even when in company. This may be due to a lack of communication, either physical or emotional.

REVERSE MEANING: The Five of Pentacles indicates the beginning of a period of bad luck where money is concerned, but this time of bad luck could be a turning point, when all aspects of your life begin to improve. It indicates change for the better and freedom from a difficult situation or relationship. You now have the ability to see where you made mistakes in the past.

RELATIONSHIP MEANING: This card suggests a relationship that is bound or restricted by financial problems. In the reversed position, it can indicate that you are overcoming financial problems, and beginning to make new plans for the future. A new job makes your financial situation more secure.

THE STORY OF THE CARD: When Cormac mac Airt, the High King of Ireland, died, the royal coffer was nearly empty. Cairpre, Cormac's son, succeeded to the throne, and decided to implement a budget to reduce the financial burden. One of the main changes was to try to reduce the high cost of keeping his band of warriors, the Fianna. At that time, each of the Fianna received a yearly tribute of 20 ingots of gold each. The Fianna refused to listen to Cairpre's pleas of poverty and demanded their yearly tribute. Cairpre decided that the only way to get out of paying was to break up the Fianna. The Fianna was made up mainly from two clans: the Clan Morna from Ulster and the Clan Baoiscne from the province of Munster. Cairpre called a great gathering of the Clans. The warriors competed with each other in mock combat, and teams from each of the clans competed in hurling games. During one of the feasts, Cairpre declared that the Clan Morna were superior in the games and better warriors in combat, knowing quite well that the Clan Baoiscne would react to this statement. Old clan rivalries came to the surface; the Fianna divided into their two clan groups and a battle took place at Gabhra. A huge number of warriors on both sides were killed. Oscar, the grandson of Fionn mac Cumhaill, led the Baoiscne clan into battle against Cairpre and the Clan Morna. Oscar and Cairpre battled with each other until both were dead and the warriors of the Fianna destroyed each other.

THE SIX OF PENTACLES
KEY WORDS

Prosperity	*Unwise Investment*
Success	*Selfishness*
Promotion	*Possessiveness*

UPRIGHT MEANING: The Six of Pentacles suggests success in business, a job promotion or a step forward in your career. It can also indicate that finance becomes available to start a business, or buy a new home. Your hard work and effort are now beginning to pay off. It also indicates that success is gained through sharing or joining with others to make a combined effort.

REVERSE MEANING: In the reversed position, it indicates that a stable period has ended. It can also suggest that greed or selfishness is restricting development and progression in a partnership or business. Team members may have different objectives and the inability to agree on a common purpose or goal creates an unhealthy environment.

RELATIONSHIP MEANING: In a relationship reading, this card indicates a sense of security. There is security in establishing a home base and a common purpose. It also indicates that success is gained through a willingness to share with each other. The Six of Pentacles represents generosity; a gift or a treat. In the reversed position, it indicates possession – that one partner may have subtle power over the other.

THE STORY OF THE CARD: Corb mac Cinian, King of Leinster, had a magic shield, which was called a Lumman. This shield had on it the image of a fierce and savage lion. This image was made of spells and ancient magic lore so powerful that none of the Kings of Ireland would face Corb in combat. The magic was so powerful that only a great warrior could handle it.

Fer Bern mac Regamna was a seer, a warrior and a poet. He was going fight in the battle of Cerna, on the side of Conn of the Hundred Battles, against the Picts of Araide. He wrote a poem in honour of Corb to ask him for a loan of the famous magic shield. It is said that 'Fer Bern was half the battle' on the side of Conn and 'bore the dint of thrice fifty blows', until he had to turn for home to seek healing for his wounds. He only managed to reach Teach Strafain (Straffan in Kildare) which was half way, and there he succumbed to his wounds. On his last dying breath, he said, 'The name of this place shall be Lumman until Doomsday.' Hence the name Lumman of Teach Strafain or Field of the Lumman, or Shield. With great sadness, Tur the charioteer buried Fer Bern with his spear on one side of him and his sword and scabbard of bronze on the other, and the magic shield covering him.

THE SEVEN OF PENTACLES
KEY WORDS

Plan carefully   *Impatience*
Invest wisely   *Bad timing*
Growth and development   *Unrealistic goals*

UPRIGHT MEANING: Success has produced just rewards and it's time to reflect and plan for the future. The situation at present is stable but you must plan carefully and invest wisely. In a relationship, it is now time to plan to lay a stable financial foundation for the future. Beware of taking financial risks, avoid 'instant riches' schemes, no matter how good they seem to be.
REVERSE MEANING: In the reversed position, the Seven of Pentacles indicates dissatisfaction or a feeling that you have lost your sense of direction. In a business or partnership question, the Seven of Pentacles indicates that the people in this partnership have unrealistic goals or that one of the partners is making a 'now or never' ultimatum. You are not able to reap what

you have sown.

RELATIONSHIP MEANING: The Seven indicates that the relationship has moved to a level where common objectives are acknowledged. You and your partner are laying down and agreeing the foundation for a financial future. Both people are content to wait for the right moment to make further investment in the future. In the reversed position, it suggests that one partner is pushing the other to make a financial commitment that he or she does not understand or is not completely happy about.

THE STORY OF THE CARD: Aengus mac Ind Og, who was a Celtic god of love and son of the Dagda, lived and held court at Brugh Na Boinne – now known as Newgrange. He was considered one of the wisest magicians of the Tuatha Dé Danann. In 'The Dream of Aengus', Aengus was regularly visited in his dreams by a beautiful, young woman who gave her name as Caer. Each time he tried to put his arms around her she vanished. This woman had such an effect on him that he became thin and ill with longing for her. His love for her became so strong that he began to let his management of his affairs completely slip. His advisers were so concerned for his wellbeing that they sent for his physicians. But even they could do nothing to relieve the effect of this woman in Aengus's dreams so they sent for the Dagda. Aengus gave the Dagda a description of this beautiful woman who was haunting his dreams and who had bewitched him. The Dagda told Aengus that the woman lived in real life somewhere in the land of Eire. Against the warnings of his advisers, Aengus gathered many search parties together and sent them to every corner of the land to find this beautiful maiden. He offered a huge financial reward for the person who found the woman. Eventually, after a year of searching, they discovered her. She was living beside a lake in County Tipperary. Her name was Caer Ibormeith, meaning Yew Berry. When Aengus saw his dream come to life, he immediately approached Caer's father and asked for permission to marry her. They married and lived happily for many years.

THE EIGHT OF PENTACLES

KEY WORDS

Craftsmanship	Poor-quality work
Employment	Despondency
Learning	Unwillingness to learn

UPRIGHT MEANING: This is a card of success; it indicates you are building on your previous success. You are always ready to learn new skills and find alternative ways to improve your quality of life and those around you. In a relationship reading, it suggests commitment to the relationship – you are prepared to put extra effort into your relationship to make it permanent. Your focus is on working, possibly too much.

REVERSE MEANING: In the reversed position, the Eight of Pentacles suggests a lack of commitment to a partnership, business or relationship. It can also indicate that you are in a job or career that is boring, repetitive and probably offering no rewards. You have become despondent and are finding it difficult to take the steps that are necessary if your environment is to improve.

RELATIONSHIP MEANING: The Eight of Pentacles in a relationship reading indicates that you are prepared to work hard to achieve the goals of the relationship. This card is very much focused on material success, for example being prepared to work together for material comfort and financial security. In the reversed position, it suggests that there is a disagreement in your relationship as to how to deal with a financial or property issue. Both partners are having difficulty in finding common financial aims.

THE STORY OF THE CARD: Goibniu was the Irish Smith God. He was a master goldsmith of the Tuatha Dé Danann, and lived as a chieftain at the High King's palace at Tara. Goibniu, along with his two brothers Luchta and Credne, collectively known as the Three Gods of Craftsmanship, forged all the weapons used by the Tuatha Dé Danann at the battle of Mag Tuired. It is believed that Goibniu fostered Lugh after his grandfather Balor abandoned him in the sea to drown. During Lugh's stay with Goibniu, Lugh learned many skills that later helped him gain access to the royal court of Tara, before the battle of Mag Tuired. It was at this battle that Lugh, originally King of the Formorians, joined the Tuatha Dé Danann and became their leader. It was Goibniu who made the magic spear that Lugh used to kill his grandfather Balor.

THE NINE OF PENTACLES
KEY WORDS

Fulfilling obligations	*Weakness of character*
Personal contentment	*Lethargy*
Success through foresight	*Lack of foresight*

UPRIGHT MEANING: Success and satisfaction come after taking on a challenge or challenges that involve taking risks. This card can suggest that you are happy, maybe because of a chance you took moving to a new home or making a change in your career. There is personal harmony and balance in your work or environment. Foresight, good planning and being prepared to take some risks brings success.

REVERSE MEANING: In reverse, the Nine of Pentacles suggests that weakness of character and lack of self-confidence bring failure and loneliness. You want success, but without having to put in any effort. It also suggests that you are not following things through to completion. You are not always prepared to take command of a particular situation.

RELATIONSHIP MEANING: In a relationship reading, it indicates that the success of a relationship is based on the material wealth and financial success achieved by either one or both people in the relationship. In the reversed position, the Nine indicates that you are only interested in how much money the other person can bring into the relationship, how much they earn or are worth in monetary terms.

THE STORY OF THE CARD: Mael Dúin set off with 17 friends in search of the killers of his father Ailill mac Owens, who had died before Mael Dúin's birth. He built a currach, a traditional boat, large enough to carry them all. Blessed by a Druid, the currach carried them to the Otherworld where they visited over 30 islands and had many adventures. On one island, they were welcomed by a queen and her 17 daughters, and treated to more delights than most mortal men could resist. The Queen promised that if they stayed, they would never age. After three months, they tried to leave. Angry at their attempts to leave, the Queen threw a magic ball of thread into the sea, causing the waves to rise so high that not even the ships of the Tuatha Dé Danann could sail over them. On their fourth attempt, the Queen threw the string as before, but this time it caught around the hand of one of the men. They cut his hand off and escaped. When they arrived at the next island, they met an old monk who converted them to Christianity. He asked Mael Dúin to forgive the man who killed his father. Mael Dúin did this and later met with his former enemies at another island, where he was given a huge welcome. He returned home after nine years and even though he did not avenge his father's death, he was satisfied that he had achieved a successful outcome with the bonus of many fabulous tales to tell from his voyage to the Otherworld.

THE TEN OF PENTACLES
KEY WORDS

Success	*Theft*
Completion	*Gambling debts*
Prosperity	*Sudden financial loss*

UPRIGHT MEANING: You feel secure, but don't get trapped by this feeling. The Ten of Pentacles is the card of success, the completion of a cycle, or the achievement of a specific set of goals or aspirations. The rewards of hard work, sacrifice and persistence against the odds have finally paid off.

The Ten of Pentacles can also indicate that success can be achieved only if all the people in the partnership or relationship are prepared to put in an equal effort and take equal risks.

REVERSE MEANING: There is success at the expense of others, or a sense of strife resulting from financial loss. There may be sudden or unexpected financial loss. Badly-managed finances create an unstable emotional or relationship situation.

RELATIONSHIP MEANING: In a relationship, the Ten of Pentacles suggests a sense of completion. Financial stability has been achieved through a long-term commitment from both partners. This is a loving relationship based on an understanding of each other's needs. Coming to terms with each other's material desires, wise decisions and a common goal have brought financial security for the people involved.

THE STORY OF THE CARD: Tigernmas, the King of Ireland in the year 1618 BC, lived by the River Liffey and was said to have reigned for 77 years. He was the first king to use gold and had standing cups made of gold and also silver, and he also had his goldsmith make pins and brooches. He established a ranking system with the use of coloured robes, and also used different types of gold and silver robe clips to distinguish rank and class. A good king to his people, Tigernmas fought many victorious battles. In one major battle, his warriors defeated the Fir Bolg, a lower race of Celtic people who invaded Ireland. During Tigernmas's reign, nine lakes erupted and three rivers burst forth causing flooding all over the country. One Samain night, while Tigernmas was worshipping Crom Cruach, a corn god who was the chief idol of adoration, a plague descended and Tigernmas and 'three-quarters of the men of Eire' died. The plague spread throughout the country. After his death, there were many glorious tributes to Tigernmas. He was remembered as a victorious warrior chief and a fair king, and was respected by all. When he died, Eire was said to be without a king for seven years.

THE PRINCESS OF PENTACLES

Astrological Key: Any Earth Sign influence
Astrological Signs: Taurus, Virgo, Capricorn

KEY WORDS

Self-discipline	*Lack of commitment*
A reliable person	*An unreliable person*
News about money	*Unwelcome news*

UPRIGHT MEANING: The image of the Princess of Pentacles is that she is a reliable person who is not easily distracted from her course of action. This card suggests good news about money, or perhaps a new job. Now is a good time to start a new job or change direction. You may be under the influence of someone who has a good sense of business or finance. Or you may have recently come into contact with a serious young person who is likely to succeed in achieving her goals and aspirations. It can also indicate the development of a relationship to a more secure level.

REVERSE MEANING: In the reversed position, the Princess of Pentacles suggests a lack of commitment, or one who has difficulty relating to others. You may soon hear unwelcome news to do with finances or property. The Princess reversed can also suggest someone who, through carelessness, lets opportunities slip through her fingers.

RELATIONSHIP MEANING: This card in a relationship position represents a young woman who is very much focused on material and financial gain. Property and financial security are more important to her in a relationship than love or emotional fulfilment. In the reversed position, it indicates a woman who feels let down because her relationship has not brought the financial rewards she originally desired.

THE STORY OF THE CARD: Banba was a queen of the Tuatha Dé Danann. She was a warrior goddess who protected Ireland from invaders and was one of three sisters, the daughters of Fiachna, who represented three aspects of Ireland. Banba symbolized the warrior aspect of Ireland: Fodla, the second of the trio, represented the spiritual side. And Eire, the third, represented the earthy or geographical aspect. Her husband was King mac Cuill, one of the last kings of the Tuatha Dé Danann before they were defeated by the Milesians. When the Milesian invaders first came to Ireland, Banba went to meet them. She used her magical powers to try to overcome them, but failed against the force of the Milesians. The Tuatha were thus defeated in battle, and forced to go to the Otherworld. However, Amergin, who was the chief bard of the Milesians, promised to name Ireland after the Triple Goddess of Banba, Fodla and Eire, so that the glory of the Tuatha Dé Danann would never be forgotten. The first two names were lost to posterity, and Ireland is still known to this very day as Eire.

THE PRINCE OF PENTACLES
Astrological Sign: Virgo
Astrological Influence: Ruled by Mercury, the planet of communication.
It is a negative, mutable Earth sign, sometimes cynical, often
pernickety, rational, cautious and realistic.

KEY WORDS

Leadership	*Irresponsible*
Opportunities	*Impatient*
Trustworthy	*Bad attitude*

UPRIGHT MEANING: When the Prince of Pentacles is drawn in a layout, it indicates the influence of a man, who may be a suitor. This man would be a good provider and family man. The Prince of Pentacles represents a person between 25 and 40 with great skills and abilities and a practical attitude. It can also indicate a man who brings practical advice. It also shows good news coming to do with financial matters. This young man is sometimes too sensible for his age.

REVERSE MEANING: The Prince in the reversed position represents a person who has potential, but lacks the self-confidence to make the most of this potential. He tends to lack imagination and generally finds himself working in boring jobs that offer long-term security. He is good with financial and planning matters and knows how to make money. But he sometimes needs to be motivated. Although he is secure and earthy, he sometimes is too stubborn for his own good.

RELATIONSHIP MEANING: Relationships for this Prince must offer security, as he lacks emotional energy and seldom makes much of an effort to improve relationships once established. In the reversed position, he seldom makes enough effort to become involved in a relationship, hence he tends to be a life-long bachelor.

THE STORY OF THE CARD: There was one very special salmon – the 'Salmon of Knowledge' – which swam the waters of the River Boyne. This salmon was said to contain the key to all knowledge, and one taste would leave a person aware of everything going on in Ireland. It was foretold that someone called Fionn would taste this special fish. A Druid teacher called Fionn lived by the River Boyne; he lived there purposely, hoping that he would be the one to taste the Salmon of Knowledge. He occupied his students in catching salmon. While cooking one of these salmon, one of his students called Deimne saw a blister on the side of the fish, pressed it down with his thumb and burnt it in the process. Jumping up with the pain, Deimne began to suck his thumb. Suddenly, he saw in his mind things that were happening in the royal courts of Tara, Emain Macha and Naas. He told the Druid, 'This cannot happen.' The Druid replied, 'Only someone called Fionn can have this wisdom, you are called Deimne.' 'Yes, but I am Fionn also,' replied Deimne,' thus named by Conn of the Hundred Battles.' From that day on, whenever Fionn needed to know something, he would press his thumb against one of his top teeth and the wisdom would come. This was how a tooth came to be named a wisdom tooth.

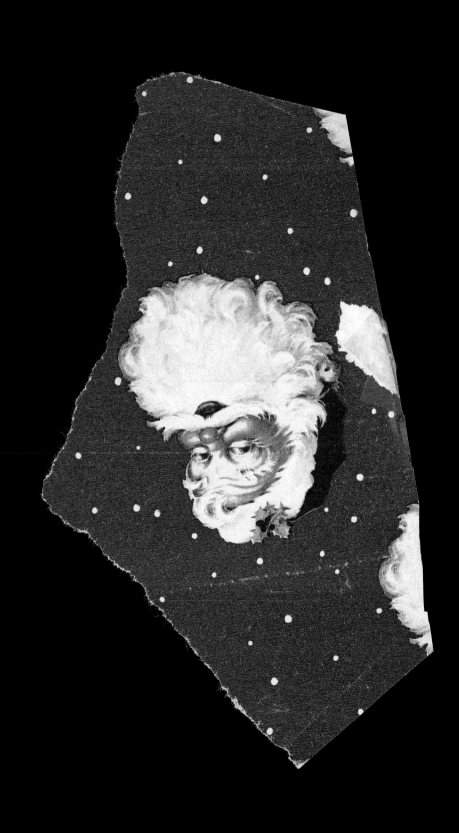

THE QUEEN OF PENTACLES

Astrological Sign: Taurus
Astrological Influence: Ruled by Venus, the planet of love. It is a
negative, fixed Earth sign, sometimes stubborn, often slow, passive,
sensual and physical.

KEY WORDS

Intelligent	*Lacks self-confidence*
Excellent taste	*Imbalance*
Patience	*Bears a grudge*

UPRIGHT MEANING: The Queen of Pentacles tends to be a socialite and enjoys entertaining. This Queen is also an excellent businesswoman. Don't be fooled by her gentle exterior, for when it comes to business she can be as hard as nails. She likes to spend her money carefully, is reliable and down to earth by nature. Her caring nature extends to all; she enjoys making others happy. Her advice is practical, and straight to the point. Because she is loyal and trusting, she will give you many opportunities to prove yourself, but if you do anything to lose that trust, you will probably never regain it.

REVERSE MEANING: The Queen in reverse indicates a woman who is greedy for money and power. She lacks self-confidence, and is out of touch with what is going on in her environment and needs to become more grounded. She sometimes lacks the ability to work for what she wants.

RELATIONSHIP MEANING: The Queen of Pentacles fits comfortably into the relationship of her choice. She is flexible and responds well to a partner who shares her sensible approach to life. She is cautious with money and an excellent businesswoman. Under pressure she keeps herself well grounded and level headed. She is loyal and generally emotionally well balanced. This card in the reversed position suggests a woman who is too cautious and has an obsession with financial security.

THE STORY OF THE CARD: Ceasair was considered by many to be the first ruler of Ireland. She probably came from Greece and belonged to a race known as the Partholonians, who were possibly a branch of Formorians. They were said to be among the first to occupy Ireland. Ceasair came to Ireland with three men (Bith, Ladra, and Fintan) and 50 women. She was the daughter of Noah, and one tale tells us that Noah refused Ceasair and Bith permission to enter the ark. They then rejected Noah's God and took an idol to worship. The idol advised them to make a ship, which they did and sailed in it for seven and a quarter years before arriving at a bay near what is now Cork City. The men and women separated into three groups, and Ceasair herself went to Connacht. One source tells us that she died by the banks of the Boyle in County Roscommon and was buried in Carn Ceasra.

THE KING OF PENTACLES
Astrological Sign: Capricorn
Astrological Influence: Ruled by Saturn, the taskmaster. It is a
negative, cardinal Earth sign, sometimes frugal, often contained,
cautious, efficient and sensible.

KEY WORDS

Intelligent	*Corruption*
Skilful	*Dishonourable behaviour*
Patience	*Dishonest businessperson*

UPRIGHT MEANING: This card represents an individual who combines knowledge and practicality to achieve his objectives. He is a builder and manager, a person who has achieved success through practical effort. The King is intelligent and enjoys earning money. Material wealth is important, yet he is caring and a good friend. Happiness for him is a comfortable lifestyle and possessions. He finds opportunity everywhere and succeeds in achieving anything he sets his mind to. Dependable and responsible, once he makes a commitment he will not let people down. The King of Pentacles is sometimes seen as the banker.

REVERSE MEANING: The King reversed suggests someone who may take risks with money without weighing up the consequences. He tends to be inconsistent in his approach to dealing with money and may be dishonest. In a relationship reading, it can indicate a person who sees his partner as a possession rather than a person.

RELATIONSHIP MEANING: The King of Pentacles can be kind and generous. He looks to his relationship for the warmth and fulfilment that is lacking in his daily business life. He is practical and cautious with money, and generous with his time and advice, which will be well founded and good to follow. The King of Pentacles marries for security and seldom makes huge emotional demands on his partner. In reverse, however, he tends to be frugal and mean with his own money, but free with yours.

THE STORY OF THE CARD: Cormac mac Airt was king of Ulster around AD 230. He was the illegitimate son of a high king. As a baby, he was separated from his mother and was suckled and raised by a pack of wolves. A hunter eventually found him and returned him to his mother. Years later, he rightly claimed his crown as High King. King Manannán mac Lir gave Cormac a present of a silver branch containing golden apples. These apples produced music that could soothe all. Cormac's reign was known as the golden age of plenty, and it is told that he reigned for 40 years. He is credited with having the history of the country recorded in one book, called the Psalter. During his reign, Cormac began to embrace the Christian religion. This caused the Druids to turn against him, fearing that the old ways would be replaced, and they placed a spell on him. Shortly after, Cormac choked to death on a salmon bone at Clettech in the Boyne valley.

THE ASTROLOGICAL
INFLUENCE OF THE
COURT CARDS

This chapter looks at the influence of the astrological Sun Signs and the Court Cards.

The four astrological elements of Fire, Earth, Water and Air relate very much to the four elements of the suits of the Tarot: Wands – Fire, Pentacles – Earth, Cups – Water and Swords – Air.

The cards of the Princesses do not relate to a specific Sun Sign, they represent the influence of the element of the specific suit, for example the Princess of Wands has the influence and qualities of the Fire Signs in general. Another influence that has to be taken into account is that represented by the Three Qualities or basic principles of life: Cardinal, Fixed and Mutable.

The Cardinal Signs represent dynamic energy, creative ability and power. Hence we associate the Kings with the Cardinal Signs of Aries, Capricorn, Cancer and Libra.

The Fixed Signs represent stability, receptivity and containment. So we associate the cards of the Queens with the Fixed Signs of Leo, Taurus, Scorpio and Aquarius.

The Mutable Signs represent flexibility, adaptability and volatility, and so we associate the Princes with the Mutable Signs of Sagittarius, Virgo, Pisces and Gemini.

When reading a Court Card try to identify if the card represents the querent, a particular aspect of the querent's personality or an attitude that will influence the querent in a positive or negative way. If it represents another person, look carefully at the position in which it is placed, and then compare it with the surrounding cards. For example, if the King of Swords is in the hopes and fears position, this may be an indication that the querent may fear the influence of the person represented by the King of Swords.

The Court Cards play an important part in a Tarot reading, because apart from personal significance, they help identify people who have played or will play an important part in the querent's life. The influence of this person may be positive or negative depending on the position of the Court Card and the other cards surrounding it. By including the astrological sign associated with the card, we are open to a lot more information that can help us identify or be on the look-out for a particular person.

Princess of Wands	Fire Sign influences
Princess of Cups	Water Sign influences
Princess of Swords	Air Sign influences
Princess of Pentacles	Earth Sign influences

Prince of Wands	Sagittarius	Mutable
Prince of Cups	Pisces	Mutable
Prince of Swords	Gemini	Mutable
Prince of Pentacles	Virgo	Mutable

Queen of Wands	Leo	Fixed
Queen of Cups	Scorpio	Fixed
Queen of Swords	Aquarius	Fixed
Queen of Pentacles	Taurus	Fixed

King of Wands	Aries	Cardinal
King of Cups	Cancer	Cardinal
King of Swords	Libra	Cardinal
King of Pentacles	Capricorn	Cardinal

WHAT IS A TAROT READING/LAYOUT/SPREAD?

A Tarot reading, layout or spread is a visual map that offers insights into personal contribution, personal motives, and conscious, subconscious and psychological influences of a particular situation or question. It is like taking a picture of a particular situation. When you take a little time to study the picture and peel away the different layers, you find that it gives you a multi-dimensional view, and many different perspectives. A layout in the hands of a competent reader can reveal an amazing amount of information. Much to the surprise of the querent, a good reading will give information of which even he or she may not be consciously aware. The motivation of the querent plays an important part in obtaining a successful outcome of a reading. You will find that there are as many different reasons for readings as there are people. Some people will come out of curiosity, some for the fun of it, and others will come with specific questions. Care must be taken that you do not let the querent take control of the reading and then guide you into giving them the answer they want. A reading can be complex and cryptic in its guidance, and it may take the querent some time to work through the message given. Because of the nature of a Tarot reading, there is a general misconception that you are there to give answers, but this is not the case. You must take great care that you don't fall into the trap of being seen as the person who gives the answers.

THE LAYOUTS

I have a preference for two particular layouts – the Celtic Cross and the Relationship Layout. I have included both in this chapter. As you might

expect, different readers or teachers of Tarot often give different interpretations for the meaning of each position. When you start reading Tarot,
you should go with the meanings I give below. Then, when you have been
reading for a while, if you intuitively feel that the meanings of the positions are different from the meanings I have given you, change to your own
definition. As I said before, you must always trust your intuitive guidance.

Preparation Before a Reading

It is only natural that you will feel nervous when you start to do a reading
for someone else, particularly if it is for someone you don't know. That is
why you should try to develop a system that helps you prepare for a reading. Your environment is very important – try to use a quiet room with
relaxing background music, candles and low light. This always helps create the right atmosphere. Buy or make a special tablecloth or piece of
material to cover your table, and only use this cloth when doing readings.
From the moment you start to set up your room and prepare your space,
you will automatically begin to prepare mentally. I like to burn a relaxing
aromatherapy oil, and clear the room of any negative energies by walking
around the room with a burning incense stick. Shuffle the cards yourself
and take a little time to reflect on some of the illustrations. And last but
not least – relax.

Doing a Reading with the Celtic Cross

The Celtic Cross is probably the most popular layout used world-wide,
though there are many variations of interpretation of the different positions in this layout. The version I give below is the one I have used for years.

Ask the querent to shuffle the cards. Let the querent decide how long
they shuffle for, as it is not important how they shuffle the cards but that
they make a solid contact with the cards. Fan the cards out in a semicircle
face down.

Now ask the querent to choose one card. This card is the Significator.
Put this card to one side facing down. (This card will be placed in position

1 in the layout plan.)

Ask the querent to choose nine more cards, placing them one on top of the other, facing down. (These cards will be placed in turn in the positions 2-10.)

Turning the Significator face up, lay it in position 1. Then lay out the other cards in positions 2 to 10 as they were chosen.

Take as much time as you need to study the cards in their positions, and how they relate to each other.

Let your intuition guide you. After a little while, a picture will start to develop in your mind. Don't be afraid to trust your feelings. A good technique for beginners is to start with the Significator and describe to the querent the attributes of this card. And so on with each of the cards in turn. Also describe what you feel the significance is of the position of the card. Now you are well on your way to completing a successful reading.

Your role is to give a clear interpretation, NOT to make decisions for the querent. The querent must be allowed do this for him or her self. A successful reading is one that gives the querent a different perspective of an issue or situation. It should reveal or clarify opportunities, negative influences, subconscious blocks such as negative past experiences, or emotional pain from the past. It may also highlight the influences of another person, people, or circumstances that are outside the querent's control.

THE CELTIC CROSS LAYOUT

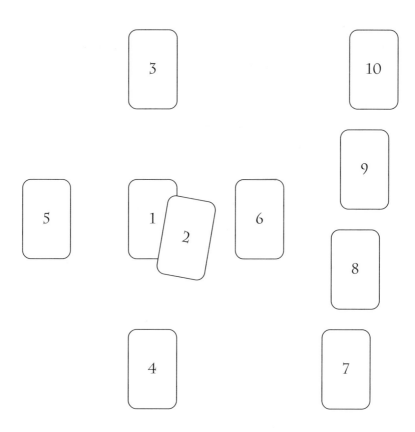

THE CELTIC CROSS LAYOUT

POSITION 1: THE SIGNIFICATOR

POSITION 2: THE COVERING CARD
This card indicates the main positive forces in the querent's favour. If this card is a negative card, it indicates obstacles that hinder progress.

Position 3: The Base Card

This card indicates the general demeanour or experience of the querent and can indicate where the querent is at present. It highlights the under-lying influences and emotional undercurrents in the querent's life.

Position 4: The Crown

This card indicates the influences that affect the thought process. This card can be viewed as messages from the 'higher self'.

Position 5: The Past Influence

This card indicates the past issues or events that colour or influence the querent's present position.

Position 6: The Challenge/ Obstacle

This card indicates the main challenges or obstacles the querent has to overcome in order to reach his or her goal.

Position 7: Psychological Influence

This position indicates the querent's psychological state and attitude to the present situation, which can affect the outcome of the matter.

Position 8: Present Environment

The card in this position represents the querent's present environment or unforeseen issues that may affect the outcome of the matter.

Position 9: Hopes and Fears

This position indicates the hopes and fears of the querent.

Position 10: Summation/ Outcome

This is the position that represents the summation or outcome of the matter.

Sample Celtic Cross Reading

John came to me for a reading. He had a number of questions he wanted to ask. Before letting John ask his questions, I decided to do a Celtic Cross layout. From a personal point of view, I prefer to do this layout before letting the client ask any questions. This layout gives a good overview of what is happening in the client's life at present. It also presents an insight into what is going on beneath the surface and helps open the psychic side of your nature, in this case allowing me to gain that intuitive sense of what was happening in John's life.

1. Two of Swords: The Significator (Where you are at present)
The first card that John chooses is the Two of Swords, indicating that at the time of the reading, John has an important decision or decisions to make. The Two of Swords also shows that John feels unsure of which direction to take. I don't know why he feels like this, until I see the other cards in the layout.

2. Moon: (What influences you at present)
The Moon represents emotions that sometimes get blown out of proportion. Depending on how they are handled, these emotions will have a major influence on the outcome. Subconscious fears presented in the Moon have to be faced alone, and dreams may be heightened during this time, as the subconscious tries to make you aware of influences hidden from view in the conscious world.

3. QUEEN OF PENTACLES (CROWN OR HEAD POSITION)

The Queen of Pentacles in the Crown position shows us that John is thinking about a woman. She is an earthy person and feels at home particularly
in the countryside. She will work hard to achieve her goals, can inspire and
help those around her and usually has good business sense.

4. THREE OF WANDS (BASE OF THE MATTER)

The Three of Wands indicates it's a time for John to consolidate his position, a time for him to prepare to put his next set of plans into action. It's
time for John to look at his present situation, and bring together everything and everybody in his environment that is positive and use them to
create a new future. The Three of Wands in this position indicates that it
is crucial that he consolidates his position now.

5. ACE OF PENTACLES (MAJOR INFLUENCE)

The Ace of Pentacles represents new beginnings, a new idea that inspires
a new perspective. It tells us that there are new ideas coming to the surface
in John's mind. Aces represent new beginnings, a spark of inspiration that
creates a whole new plan for the future. In this position the Ace shows us
that John has new plans in his mind, a new perspective, that will affect his
work and love life and if handled correctly will bring about a positive outcome.

6. FIVE OF WANDS (CHALLENGE POSITION)

The challenge position highlights what John see as the issues or obstacles
in his present environment. The Five of Wands represents conflict, although
this conflict is not serious enough to harm anyone. In this position, it tells
us that John has been resisting the idea of attempting to resolve the issues
that have to be sorted out one way or the other. This card in this position
also tells us that John is well capable of facing up to the challenges of the
present moment and bringing about a successful outcome.

7. THE SUN (PSYCHOLOGICAL POSITION)

The card of the Sun in the psychological position shows that it is time to take on board a more optimistic attitude. It is a time to know the value of friendship in a relationship, and the opportunities there to be taken in the present moment. The Sun draws on the inner strength found in the Strength card, and the ability to surrender to the change indicated in the Death card.

8. EIGHT OF PENTACLES (ENVIRONMENT POSITION)

This card suggests a deeper commitment to a person or situation. In John's case it embraces both. It is also the card of learning new skills, the need and the ability to bring together all the ingredients that are available in the present time to create something new.

9. TEN OF CUPS (HOPES AND FEARS POSITION)

This position has two very distinct sides to it – the positive and the negative. Both are embraced in the one position. On the positive side, the Ten of Cups shown us that John wishes for fulfilment in a relationship. On the other side, however, he also has the fear that if he commits himself it may not work.

10. TEN OF PENTACLES (OUTCOME)

The Ten of Pentacles depicts an excellent outcome for John. This card shows a solid foundation and structure in his future life, financial security and a relationship environment in balance and harmony. It also shows a relationship linked to his career, a dynamic combination that brings success in a relationship and business.

John is 31, self-employed since he was 20. His business is successful, but not fulfilling for him anymore. John feels that he has been stuck in a rut for some time. He has been in a relationship with Elaine for the last two years and they love each other very much. John feels that recently Elaine has been making overtures about taking their relationship to the next stage. John would like to do that, but has had a fear of making a total commitment to the relationship. In the recent past, new ideas for developing his business have come to mind, and in discussing these ideas with Elaine, she surprised him with her business acumen. John now wonders if it would be a good idea not only to propose to Elaine, but also to invite her to join the business.

Looking back over John's layout, we can see clearly that the Two of Swords shows John's uncertainty, covered by the card of the Moon indicating a strong flow of emotions. The Ace and the Queen of Pentacles show the positive influence of John's new ideas, backed by Elaine's clear and positive ability to see John's situation from a different perspective. We also see that if John is prepared to follow his natural instincts, both he and Elaine have an excellent future to look forward to.

SHORT RELATIONSHIP LAYOUT

This is a new layout that I have developed for people who are in a relationship and would like to take a look at the relationship from the perspective of both partners. It is done as a reading that is usually performed for one person, but it takes into account both that person and their partner in a relationship.

As the name suggests, it is only intended to give an overview – not an in-depth interpretation. However, it can give a good insight as to how both partners see this relationship and what their individual aspirations are with regard to the relationship. Although this is a relationship reading, it is usually done for only one person, that is only one person chooses the cards.

Although this layout is only an overview of the relationship, it can be very worthwhile in that it highlights the main goals of each partner, where they see the relationship going, and what issues and attitudes they may have to face.

With regard to the sample layout below, we'll call our couple A and B

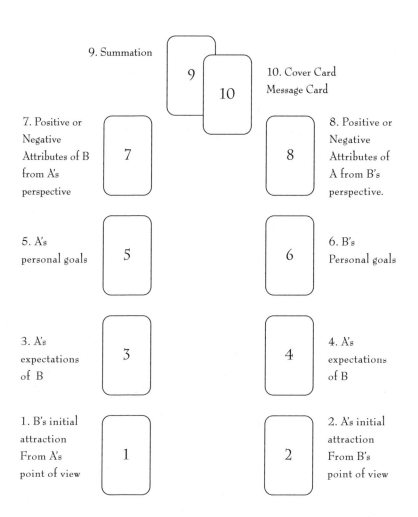

9. Summation

10. Cover Card
Message Card

7. Positive or
Negative
Attributes of B
from A's
perspective

8. Positive or
Negative
Attributes of
A from B's
perspective.

5. A's
personal goals

6. B's
Personal goals

3. A's
expectations
of B

4. A's
expectations
of B

1. B's initial
attraction
From A's
point of view

2. A's initial
attraction
From B's
point of view

POSITION 1: HOW A SEES B
This position suggests how A sees B, or what particular qualities B has that
initially attracted A to B.

POSITION 2: HOW B SEES A
This position suggests how B sees A, or what particular qualities A has that
initially attracted B to A.

POSITION 3: A's PRESENT EXPECTATIONS
This position indicates what A expects to get out of the relationship - where A sees the relationship in the present and short term future.

POSITION 4: B's PRESENT EXPECTATIONS
This position indicates what B expects to get out of the relationship – where A sees the relationship in the present and short-term future.

POSITION 5: A's PERSONAL GOALS IN TERMS OF THE RELATIONSHIP
This position shows how A sees this relationship developing in the long term – what A's personal goals are in terms of the relationship.

POSITION 6: B's PERSONAL GOALS IN TERMS OF THE RELATIONSHIP
This position shows how B sees this relationship developing in the long term – what B's personal goals are in terms of the relationship.

POSITION 7: WHAT A CONSIDERS B's POSITIVE OR NEGATIVE ATTITUDES TO BE
This position highlights what positive or negative attitudes A feels that B is bringing to the relationship – attitudes that will help or hinder the relationship from developing in the way that A wants it to.

POSITION 8: WHAT B CONSIDERS A's POSITIVE OR NEGATIVE ATTITUDES TO BE
This position highlights what positive or negative attitudes B feels A is bringing to the relationship – attitudes that will help or hinder the relationship from developing in the way that B wants it to.

POSITION 9: CONCLUSION
This card gives an indication of the possible outcome of the relationship. Of course, when we look at this card for a conclusion, we also have to take into account the personal goals of both people in the relationship. We also need to consider the cards in Positions 7 and 8 that may highlight stumbling blocks that need to be sorted out in order for the relationship to

develop in a meaningful way. And of course, we need to take into account the message from the card in Position 10.

POSITION 10: MESSAGE CARD

This card is the Message Card – it tells us of something important to consider within the relationship; something that may not show up as either partner's goals or aspirations, but simply something that needs to be taken into account if the relationship is to reach its full potential.

SAMPLE READING

During a recent reading for Ann, she asked if we could look at her relationship with Robert. They had worked together as designers for the same company for two years before their relationship developed beyond the platonic stage. They have been romantically involved now for eight months.

POSITION 1: WHAT ANN INITIALLY SAW IN ROBERT

THE KING OF WANDS

This card suggests that Ann was initially attracted by Robert's confidence and the way he takes on new challenges, particularly in work. She admires his creative ability and enjoys working with him. As a designer herself, she feels that they would have the potential to be very successful both as a work team and as partners.

POSITION 2: WHAT ROBERT INITIALLY SAW IN ANN

THE LOVERS

This card indicates that Robert's initial attraction to Ann was a physical one. It would suggest a sexual attraction from his point of view, rather than suggesting that in the early stages he was seeking a long-term relationship. Ann said that Robert had recently told her that before they got involved, he had fancied her for months, but hadn't done anything about it because he was wary of having a relationship with someone he worked with.

POSITION 3: ANN'S PRESENT EXPECTATIONS
SIX OF PENTACLES
This card suggests that Ann desires security in a relationship. Although they have only been together for eight months, she feels that this relationship could be very long-term for her. She hopes that Robert has the same level of commitment and that they will move on to the next stage, that is a sense of common purpose: establishing a home base together.

POSITION 4:   ROBERT'S PRESENT EXPECTATIONS
TWO OF CUPS
This card suggests that Robert feels that this relationship is still in the early stages. The two people involved have a lot to offer each other, to build on for the future. It may be the time for the first pledging of love to each other for the present and also for the future. This is the time to let the foundation of love grow into something special. However, if it was in the reversed position, it would suggest a time of emotionally charged quarrels – perhaps that Robert is questioning the value of the relationship and his commitment to it.

POSITION 5: ANN'S PERSONAL GOALS IN TERMS OF THE RELATIONSHIP
TEN OF CUPS
Ann feels that this relationship has all the right ingredients for success. There is a stable environment and happiness is forecast. Ann is committed to Robert and feels that they have a trusting, honest and satisfying relationship.

POSITION 6: ROBERT'S PERSONAL GOALS IN TERMS OF THE RELATIONSHIP
NINE OF PENTACLES
Robert feels that this relationship has the basis for a long-term commitment. He also feels that they could combine their energies and skills to create a financially secure environment. He feels comfortable in the relationship, and sees the possibility in the future of bringing a business aspect

to their relationship. He feels that they would make a good working team.

POSITION 7: WHAT ANN CONSIDERS ROBERT'S POSITIVE OR NEGATIVE ATTITUDES
TO BE

PRINCE OF WANDS

Ann's main fear in the relationship is that Robert will put his career first and will not make the necessary commitment to their relationship for the long term. She realizes that he is ambitious, but hopes that he can combine a progressive career and a loving relationship with her.

POSITION 8: WHAT ROBERT CONSIDERS ANN'S POSITIVE OR NEGATIVE ATTITUDES
TO BE

THREE OF CUPS

This card suggests that Robert may fear that Ann will want a commitment from him before he is ready to give one. It does not mean that he does not want to commit to this relationship, but that he may not be ready just yet to do so.

POSITION 9: CONCLUSION

TWO OF PENTACLES

The Two of Pentacles in this position suggests that Ann and Robert's relationship has the potential to develop, but they need to sit down and discuss openly and honestly what they both want and expect from this relationship, rather than just letting the relationship drift along. I feel that financial security is a very important aspect of this relationship, but I also think that this is a good possibility as Ann and Robert work together very well.

POSITION 10: MESSAGE CARD

THE HANGED MAN

The Hanged Man in a relationship reading symbolizes the self-sacrifice that is sometimes required to make a relationship work. The Hanged Man's message for Ann is that Robert's career will always be very important to him. At times, he may seem to put it before her. However, it is not that he is putting Ann second, but that he sees his career as the important foundation for a long-term, successful relationship.

CONCLUSION

This was quite a positive reading in terms of Ann and Robert's relationship. Ann needs to let Robert commit himself in his own time and not rush him into making a commitment before he is ready. And Robert needs to make sure that he doesn't spend so much time creating a secure financial base that he forgets about Ann and her needs in this relationship. If they make a point of having open, honest discussions about how they both feel, then I think that they have a very positive future together.

DOING A SHORT RELATIONSHIP LAYOUT

Ask the querent to hold the deck of cards for a couple of minutes and imagine in his or her mind an image of the querent's partner and then shuffle the cards. Let the querent decide how long they shuffle for, as it is not important how they shuffle or mix the cards, but that they make a solid contact with the cards. Now fan the cards out in a semicircle face down.

Now ask the querent to choose nine more cards, placing them one on top of the other, facing down (these cards will be placed in turn in the positions 1–10).

Take as much time as you need to study the cards in their positions. I often tell the querent in advance that I will need a few minutes to study the cards. Often they become concerned and think that when you pause for a few minutes there is something bad indicated in the layout.

Remember that you are interpreting for two specific people, whose lives are intertwined, and try to get a sense of where both people are coming from, that is what they are bringing into the relationship. What do they want from the relationship? Let your intuition guide you. After a little while, a picture will start to develop in your mind. Don't be afraid to trust your feelings.

Your role is to give a clear and honest interpretation, NOT to make decisions for the querent. The querent must be allowed do this for him or her self. A successful reading is one that gives the querent a different perspective of an issue or situation. It should reveal or clarify opportunities, negative influences, subconscious blocks such as negative past experiences, or emotional pain from the past. It may also highlight the influences of another person, other people, or circumstances that are outside the querent's control.

KEEPING RECORDS

It will be well worth your while keeping records of your readings, both practice and actual ones. Try to enlist as many friends as possible to participate in your trials. You will need people who will come to you for a number of readings over a period of time. You will need people who will be open and honest with you, and who will give you feedback as to how accurate your readings are. I have kept records for many years now and find it very helpful. Most times I keep the name in code to ensure confidentiality. An example of my records would be as follows:

NAME: Stephen
DATE: 03/05/98
PLACE: Home
                   Used background music, candles, low lights
TYPE OF LAYOUT: Celtic Cross

List of cards:
Significator   Four of Wands
Position 2   Temperance
Position 3   Knight of Cups
Position 4   Four of Swords
Position 5   Two of Cups
Position 6   Ace of Wands
Position 7   Ace of Cups
Position 8   Queen of Pentacles
Position 9   Ten of Pentacles
Position 10   Six of Swords

INTERPRETATION: The reading focused on two areas. The first suggested that there was a career opportunity coming soon. Stephen was surprised by this observation and said that he was happy in his present position and had not applied for any other positions within or outside his present company. He also said that he was not aware of any opportunities in his present company at the moment. The second suggested that Stephen would like to take his relationship with Chantal to the next stage and make a greater commitment. Stephen agreed with this interpretation, but he was uncertain about how Chantal felt. The Queen of Pentacles drawn in the environment position suggested to me that Chantal was more settled in her relationship with Stephen than he realized, and that she in turn was probably being just as cautious as Stephen.

Date: 12.08.98

FEEDBACK: Shortly after his reading, Stephen found the courage to have a serious chat with Chantal. Much to Stephen's surprise, Chantal agreed with Stephen that they should make a more serious commitment. She said that she did not want Stephen to feel pressurized within their relationship and wanted to find out for himself how he felt and where he wanted the relationship to go. They have recently decided to move into their own apartment. Two weeks ago Stephen's supervisor gave notice that he had been offered a position with a different company and Stephen has applied for the position of supervisor.

This is not the end of the book, just the beginning of your journey. Like the Fool as he starts on his new journey, look forward with an open and optimistic attitude, embrace the Magician, listen to the High Priestess, and you will seldom go wrong.